M000215062

THE WAY
TO WEALTH
IN ACTION

Building a Highly
Profitable Business

THE WAY TO WEALTH IN ACTION

Building a Highly Profitable Business

BRIAN TRACY

EP
Entrepreneur.Press

Editorial Director: Jere Calmes
Cover Design: Beth Hansen-Winter
Production and Editorial Services: CWL Publishing Enterprises, Inc.,
Madison, Wisconsin, www.cwlpub.com

© 2007 by Entrepreneur Media, Inc. and Brian Tracy

All rights reserved.
Reproduction of any part of this work beyond that permitted by
Section 107 or 108 of the 1976 United States Copyright Act without the
express permission of the copyright owner is unlawful. Requests for
permission or further information should be addressed to the Business
Products Division, Entrepreneur Media, Inc.

This publication is designed to provide accurate and authoritative
information in regard to the subject matter covered. It is sold with the
understanding that the publisher is not engaged in rendering legal,
accounting, or other professional services. If legal advice or other
expert assistance is required, the services of a competent professional
person should be sought.
—From a Declaration of Principles jointly adopted by a
Committee of the American Bar Association and
a Committee of Publishers and Associations

ISBN   13: 978-1-59918-132-5
       10: 1-59918-132-0

Library of Congress Cataloging-in-Publication Data

Tracy, Brian.
  The way to wealth in action / by Brian Tracy.
    p. cm.
  ISBN-13: 978-1-59918-132-5 (alk. paper)
  ISBN-10: 1-59918-132-0 (alk. paper)
  1. Success in business. 2. Marketing. 3. Management. 4. Profit.
I. Title.
  HF5386.T814235 2007
  658.4'09—dc22

                                                    2007023418

11 10 09 08 07   10 9 8 7 6 5 3 2 1

Printed in Canada

DEDICATION

This book is lovingly dedicated to my children and their partners, Christina and Damon, Michael and Tasha, David and Sara, and Catherine. You are the entrepreneurs and business builders of the future, and the focal points of all my hopes and aspirations for success and happiness.

CONTENTS

Contents

Contents

Contents

Contents

Turbocharging Your Business

W elcome to the second stage on your journey to wealth as an entrepreneur! I am assuming that you have already read the first book in this series, *The Way to Wealth: Part One—The Journey Begins*. This book is the continuation of those principles and ideas.

When I started out, I did not graduate from high school. I worked at laboring jobs for several years until I found myself in sales, and eventually in entrepreneurship. I struggled and suffered financially for years until I started asking and answering the question, "Why are some people more successful than others?"

What I found was that success is not an accident. It is based on practical, proven principles that have been learned and relearned for hundreds of years. As my friend Og Mandino once told me, "The great secret of success is that there are no secrets of success, just universal principles that have to be discovered over and over again by each person."

In my 30s, I invested several years and thousands of hours

in an MBA degree from a top university. Most of what I learned was theoretical and impractical in the real world. The courses, as interesting as they were at times, were taught by people who had never worked in a business in their lives.

But one of the courses stood out: Probability Theory. This course, based on differential calculus, taught two key principles. First, it taught that there is a probability that anything can happen. And second, that these probabilities can by calculated with considerable accuracy.

In other words, success in business is not based on "luck." Instead, it is based on probabilities. This means simply that, if you do the same things that successful entrepreneurs do, over and over again, you will eventually master the skills of money-making, and get the same results that they do. Your success is virtually guaranteed by learning and practicing the "secrets of success."

Earning Your Degree

When I was twenty, I began the study and practice of karate. I trained six days a week, eventually competed in four national championships and earned my black belt. Forever after, I have viewed karate as a metaphor for life, and especially business life.

You start off knowing nothing. In Zen Buddhism, this is called "no mind." You are wide open to learning, rather than being convinced that you know already.

Into this empty mind, like an empty vessel, knowledge is poured. You learn how to stand all over again. Then, you learn how to move, forward and backward. You learn how to move your arms, legs, hands and feet. Finally, you learn how to use your whole body in a new way, leading to free form exercises, called "katas," and moving onto free fighting, called "kumite."

Entrepreneurship is very much the same. It requires an entirely new set of mental skills, like learning a new language. Each lesson requires effort, and each mistake causes pain, usually financially pain. But over time, you become smarter and faster. You do more things right than wrong. You make more money, and lose less.

In the first book, you earned your "undergraduate degree" in money-making as an entrepreneur. In this book, you will take your "graduate degree." Just as in karate, you learn more and more of the small subtleties and movements as you progress from belt to belt, in business, you become better and smarter with experience and feedback. And just as in karate, there are no cheap, easy lessons. You have to pay for every step forward.

Expand Your Vocabulary

Earlier I asked the question, "What is the highest paid work in business?" The answer is "thinking!"

Why? Because the quality of your thinking determines the quality of your choices and decisions, which largely determines your income and your success. The better you think about the critical elements of your business, the more money you make.

What then is the importance of "words" in human life? The usual answer is, "to communicate." This is true, but it is not the most important aspect of word knowledge.

Words are actually "condensed thoughts." They are tools of thought and expression. And what experts have found for more than 50 years is that, the more words you know, the better you can think. The more words you know, the more complex the thoughts and ideas you can form. As a result, by learning more words, you become like a karate expert who knows more kicks, punches, blocks and movement than a less experienced opponent.

In *The Road to Wealth: Part One*, you learn the key words, concepts, ideas and thinking patterns of successful entrepreneurs. In this book, *The Way to Wealth in Action*, you learn an advanced vocabulary of ideas, methods and techniques in the field of business and entrepreneurship.

You have now learned how to succeed at a far higher level than your competitors. Now you are ready for the "advanced program" that will make you a champion in business for the rest of your career. You are now ready to make a "quantum leap" down the road to wealth.

Let us start with the most important people of all, our customers.

CHAPTER ONE

Winning the Hearts and Minds of Your Customers

The person who goes farthest is generally the one who is willing to do and dare. The sure-thing boat never gets far from shore.

—*Dale Carnegie*

The way you are positioned in the minds and hearts of your prospects and customers largely determines how easily you sell, how much you sell, how often customers buy from you, and whether or not they recommend you to others.

This positioning message can be developed inadvertently or accidentally in the course of your business—or you can specifically and deliberately decide exactly how you want your customers to think about you when your name comes up in conversation.

The most successful companies, large and small, give a lot

of thought to their positioning. They do not let the way their customers think about them be determined by chance or by accident. They decide in advance what their positioning will be. Then they make sure that everything they do in their interactions with customers repeats and reinforces this key message.

Who Are You, Ideally?

Imagine that one of your good customers calls you up one day to ask for your advice. He says, "A friend of mine called me and invited me for lunch tomorrow. He says that he is thinking about buying from you and your company, and he wants to ask me for my opinion based on my experience with you. What do you want me to say?"

If one of your customers were meeting with one of your prospects and you could write out a cue card that your customer would recite to your prospect, what words would you use?

If you could be a fly on the wall while one of your customers was describing you, your business, and your products or services to a prospect, what would you want to hear?

> If you could be a fly on the wall while one of your customers was describing you, your business, and your products or services to a prospect, what would you want to hear?

Would you want one of your customers to describe you by saying the following? "This is an excellent company. Their products and services are of superb quality. Their customer service is excellent. Their people are warm, friendly, fast, and efficient. They are people of the highest integrity. I would wholeheartedly recommend that you buy from them. You'll be happy that you did."

Is this what you would like your customers to say about you? If it is, what would you have to do, in every customer interaction, to ensure that your customers talk about you like this every time your name is mentioned?

The Critical Determinant of Success

All of marketing is *differentiation*. Everything you do in the design of your products and services, in the way you advertise and promote them, and in the way you sell and deliver them revolves around differentiating yourself from your competition.

To be successful in business, to move more rapidly along the road to wealth, your products must be different, better, and superior in one or more clear, specific ways that represent real value to your customer. You absolutely have to possess an "area of excellence" that people know, understand, recognize, and respond to.

You must have a *unique selling proposition*, something that you do or offer to your customer that is of benefit to him or her that no other competitor can offer except you. What is it for you and your product?

Be Clear About Your Target

In deciding how you will position yourself in your market, begin with your ideal customers. Who are they? Why do they buy? What do they consider value? What specific benefits are they seeking from purchasing your product or service? What do your ideal customers have to be convinced of before they will buy from you?

Who are your competitors? Why do your ideal customers buy from your competitor rather than from you? What value do your customers perceive in the offerings of your competitors that they do not perceive in your offerings? What are the most attractive features and benefits that your competitors offer that your prospective customers do not feel that you offer? What are their strengths? How have your competitors succeeded up until now? What are they doing to keep people from buying your products and services?

Once you are clear about your ideal customers and what they want, and you are clear about your competitors and why your customers are buying from your competitors, you can then analyze and dissect your product or service in more detail.

What Do You Sell?

What exactly do you sell? Remember: customers do not care what your product *is* as much as they care about what your product *does*. Customers are demanding, discerning, discriminating, and disloyal. They will buy from whichever company they feel will satisfy their specific needs of the moment better than anyone else.

And as you know, the customer is always right. The customer's decision is always *rational* in that it is based on his or her assessment of the advantages and disadvantages of each product or service that is available to satisfy his or needs. To win customers, you have to get inside their heads and view your product or service from their perspective. It is only when you can get customers to see your product or service as the best choice for them that you can make more sales.

> To win customers, you have to get inside their heads and view your product or service from their perspective.

Perception of Quality

In every business or industry, the top 20 percent of companies earn 80 percent of the profits. For this reason, thousands of companies have been studied for many years in an attempt to determine the specific factors that lead to greater growth and prosperity, as opposed to average growth or even decline or bankruptcy.

One of the most important discoveries of the Profit Impact of Marketing Strategy (PIMS) Study at Harvard, covering 620 companies over a 20-year period, was that the *perceived* level of *quality* of a company's products and services was the critical factor in determining its sales, growth, and profitability.

In other words, if a survey asked customers in a community to rate all the companies in an industry on a scale of one to ten, the company that customers rated the highest would also turn out, upon examination of their financial statements, to be the most profitable in that industry.

Each market and each product or service in a market can be divided into segments. These segments refer to the products or services themselves and to the types of customers who purchase these products or services. Because of this segmentation, it is possible for a company that sells a low-priced product to achieve the highest quality ranking in a particular market segment.

Tiffany sells high-priced jewelry and other products primarily to wealthy people for whom price is not a concern. Among quality jewelers, Tiffany has an extremely high quality ranking and is, by extension, a very profitable enterprise.

Zales Jewelers is a national chain that sells to middle-income earners. Its stores have a wide selection of engagement rings, wedding rings, and other forms of jewelry that family members and friends buy for each other. In its market segment, it has a high quality ranking in serving its particular type of customers and has therefore been highly profitable year after year.

McDonald's can certainly not be compared to a first-class restaurant, but in its market segment McDonald's is famous for excellent-quality fast food. This explains why the company is so successful and profitable in the fast-food market.

Determine Your Quality Ranking

If someone conducted a survey to determine the quality ranking of your company in your market, where would you score? It would be nice if your answer was "number one," but this may not be true, at least for the moment.

What is most important is that you determine your relative quality ranking at the current time. Let us say that, out of ten companies in your business that are attempting to sell to very much the same customers, your quality ranking is six. If you could examine the financial statements of your competitors, you would probably find that your level of profitability ranks you about the same.

Move Up One Rank

Your job now is not necessarily to be number one in your market. That is often too much of a leap. That should be your ultimate goal—to be in the top 10 percent in your industry and, ideally, to be the best. Your goal at this point is simply to improve your quality ranking by *one level*, to move from number six to number five. You can do this in the foreseeable future.

What would you have to do, starting today, to improve the way that customers think about you and talk about you when your name comes up or when they describe you to other people? What should you do first? What should you do second? What would be your plan to improve your quality ranking?

To move your company up *one* quality ranking, you must know exactly why other companies are above you on the scale. One of the best ways to find this out is to ask people who are not now your customers why they prefer to buy from your competitors rather than from you. What value do they perceive? What differences do they see between your business and your competitors?

Be curious and open, not defensive or dismissive. Ask questions and listen carefully until you know exactly what it is that your competitors' customers consider value that you are not currently offering.

Resolve to Be the Best

Every company needs values, a vision, a purpose, and a mission. Every company and everyone within it need something to aspire to. And there is nothing more motivational or inspirational in a company than for the owner to be committed to ultimately *be the best* in the industry.

There is nothing that will attract better people to join your company and bring higher-quality work out of your employees than for you to be wholeheartedly determined to get better and better in what you do until your customers ultimately rank you as "the best in the business."

Your Most Valuable Asset

As mentioned earlier in this book, according to Harvard University, the most valuable asset that a company has is its *reputation*. This is best defined as "how you are known to your customers."

Because the credibility of your advertising and your offerings is the critical determinant of whether or not people buy from you, your reputation is more important than any other single factor.

The most powerful form of advertising in our society is word-of-mouth. This takes place when your satisfied customers tell your prospective customers how good you are and how much they enjoy doing business with you.

> The most powerful form of advertising in our society is word-of-mouth.

Word-of-mouth advertising is *free*. It comes as the result of your providing excellent products and services to your customers and then taking care of your customers with excellent follow-up service.

People are generally reluctant to tell their friends and associates to patronize a particular business. They are afraid that, if they recommend a business, those friends and associates will be disappointed if they do not get what they expected from the business.

For this reason, the highest and best form of promotion is for you to take wonderful care of your customers, every single time. It takes a long time to build a reputation for excellent customer service, but once you have established it, it can help you to attract more and better business than anything else you can do.

There are some companies that are extremely successful, but do very little advertising. Instead, they focus all of their efforts on taking such great care of their customers that these customers not only return and buy again, but also tell everyone how good the business is.

It's estimated that a happy customer will tell five to eight other prospective customers about a product or service. On the other hand, an unhappy customer will tell ten to 15 people *not* to buy that product or service.

In advertising there is a rule: "Never advertise a bad product." The reason for this rule is simple. If you promote a bad product, more people will buy it, sooner. And the more people who buy it who are dissatisfied, the more people they will tell about their experience. In no time at all, the bad product will have such a bad reputation that it will quickly fail in the market. No one will buy it.

Salespeople Are Expected to Exaggerate

In commercial law, there are several reasons for setting aside a sale.

The first is *fraudulent misrepresentation*. This occurs when a salesperson says that a product or service will do something that is clearly false. Virtually any sale can be set aside if fraudulent representation can be demonstrated.

The second reason for setting aside a sale is *innocent misrepresentation*. This occurs when the salesperson says that a product will do something that it cannot do, but the salesperson genuinely believed what he or she said. In this case, the sale can still be set aside as invalid.

There is a third area in commercial law called *sales puffing*. This is a legal term that refers to the tendency of salespeople to use superlatives in describing a product or service, e.g., "This is the best, fastest, easiest, most popular, cheapest" and so on.

When a customer attempts to have a sale set aside because the salesperson exaggerated the qualities of the product or service, the court will rule that the sale is still valid. The salesperson has merely engaged in puffing. The court will rule that this is a normal part of sales activities and is to be expected. If the customer bought on the basis of puffing, then the customer is subject to what is called "caveat emptor"—"let the buyer beware."

The point is that customers are accustomed to puffing. They expect it as a normal and natural part of the sales conversation. They expect the salesperson to describe the product or service in the most positive way possible without engaging in fraudulent or innocent misrepresentation.

For this reason, whatever the salesperson says about the product or service is immediately *discounted* by customers, based on their previous experience. But when someone other than a salesperson, someone outside the company, says that your product or service is good, that statement has a high level of credibility. A skeptical customer can believe and accept a third-party testimonial.

When the movie *Seabiscuit* came out in 2003, it was based on the book of the same name, which was a bestseller. Apparently many movie critics had read the book and did not feel that the movie followed the book with sufficient accuracy. As a result, the critics wrote a series of mediocre reviews that were picked up and reprinted in newspapers across the country. The movie was rated only two stars on a four-star scale, which translates into a "Fair" rating.

But when the movie hit the theaters and people began to see it, something unexpected happened. People began telling their friends and going back to see it again.

I was part of this phenomenon. Having read the reviews and believed them, I had no intention of seeing the movie. But when my daughter told me that it was really excellent and that I would enjoy it very much, I decided to take a chance—and I'm glad I did.

By the time I got to the theater, about three weeks after its release, on a Saturday afternoon, when you would normally expect attendance to be tapering off for a movie that had only a "Fair" rating, the theater was almost full. People were pouring in, in the middle of the afternoon, to see the movie. And we were not disappointed. *Seabiscuit* is a wonderful, inspiring film that you can watch over and over again and enjoy anew each time.

Here is the interesting part. As people began to pour into the theaters to see the movie and its reputation grew across the country, the critics who had initially sneered at the movie went back and rewrote their reviews, upgrading the movie to "Good," and even "Excellent." The quality reputation of the movie turned it into a major success.

This "reputation factor" often happens with a small restaurant that opens on a side street but serves excellent food. First, a couple of people stop in to eat. Then more and more try it. As people patronize the restaurant, the restaurant becomes more and more popular. Soon it gets written up in the newspapers and local magazines and becomes a major financial success for its owner. Reputation is everything.

What Reputation Do You Want?

What kind of a reputation do you want to have for your business and for your products and services? What do you want customers to say about your products and services? How do you want people to talk about you on the street corner when your name comes up? What can you do, starting today, to ensure that people think and talk about you the same way, every single time?

Al Ries and Jack Trout, in their best-selling book, *Positioning: The Battle for Your Mind*, emphasized the importance of *owning* certain words in the customers' mind. As it happens, customers have narrow perspectives and limited viewpoints on a particular product or service. They don't describe a business with a whole series of words, but usually only one or two. What are the one or two words that you want to "own" in your customer's mind?

Every successful company owns certain words. It's just like the Pavlovian response: you show a dog a piece of meat and ring a bell and the dog salivates; then later, all you have to do is to ring the bell and the dog salivates by association. This is the same with customers: when certain words are used, certain companies immediately come to mind. And often, buying desire is triggered.

Mercedes-Benz owns the words "Quality Engineering." BMW cars own the words "Ultimate Driving Machine." Ray Kroc chose the words "Quality, Service, Cleanliness, and Value" to describe everything McDonald's did when it served its customers. Nordstrom stores immediately trigger the thought, "Excellent customer service." Rolex Watch chose to own the word "Success": to differentiate itself from the many high-quality Swiss watchmakers, the company positioned its products as the watches that people wear when they become successful. This is a very clever strategy.

Study Your Competition

To determine the words that you want to own in your customers' minds, you must first determine the words that your competitors own. It is almost impossible to elbow your way into the market with a "me too" strategy. You must choose different words.

If your competitor has a reputation for "high quality," you can then position yourself as "fast, friendly service." Customers are very discerning. They will soon figure out that your products and services are of high quality. You don't have to compete for that position when someone else already has it.

Here is a good exercise for you. Hire someone who does not work for your company to phone several of your customers, identifying himself or herself as a private pollster, and tell those customers that you are conducting a market survey to determine the perceptions that customers have of certain businesses in the community. You give your pollster a list of five competitors and your business. For each of those six businesses, you have your pollster ask two questions:

1. How would you rank this company in terms of quality on a scale of one to ten?
2. When you think of this company, what words immediately come to mind?

It takes less than an hour to conduct this complete survey and this information can be priceless to you in improving your quality ranking. It can give you a sharp, clear picture of where you stand in the marketplace relative to your competitors. It can tell you why your customers are buying from your competitors rather than from you. It can also tell you how you are perceived by your customers and the real reasons they've decided to buy from you, rather than from someone else.

Many companies get results they did not expect. They are often surprised to find that the reason customers are buying from them is different from what they thought. They may have been advertising high quality, but their customers buy from them because of the friendly service. They may have been promoting a complete selection of products, but the reason customers are buying from them is because they specialize in one or two areas.

Sometimes, the answers to a quick survey like this can not only change your marketing and advertising strategy, but also dramatically increase your sales and profitability. The results can show you how to attract more customers more easily than before.

Quality Ranking and Reputation Go Together

Your quality ranking is a core element in your reputation. The two go together. As you improve your quality ranking, your reputation improves. As your reputation improves, customers perceive you to be a higher-quality choice.

The Harvard PIMS researchers noticed an anomaly in the studies that they did not understand. They found that in the car repair part of the survey, for example, "Joe's Garage" might have received a higher quality ranking than "McArthur's Precision Automobiles." As a result of this discrepancy, they revisited the participants in the survey and asked them for their definition of "quality."

What they found was that quality was defined by customers as consisting of *two* elements.

Quality, Part One

First, quality referred to the actual product or service. Philip Crosby, founder of the Crosby Quality College, once said that the quality of your product can be defined as "the product does what you sold it to do and it continues doing it without breaking down."

A quality product works. It performs the function that you said it would perform when you sold it. It gets the results that you said it would get when the customer bought it. Like the slogan that Timex Watches used for a half century, "It takes a licking and keeps on ticking." This is the first definition of quality.

> **M**ost of your problems with customers will occur when your customers buy a product or service from you and then fail to get the result that they expected.

Most of your problems with customers will occur when your customers buy a product or service from you and then fail to get the result that they expected. Your product or service does not do what it was sold to do. Your product or service breaks down and stops performing the function for which it was bought. This causes your customers to be frustrated, disappointed, and angry.

Surveys of thousands of dissatisfied customers found that unhappy customers did not want their money back. They did not want to sue. All they wanted was for the product you sold them to perform as you had told them it would. They just wanted to be "made whole." They were not unreasonable or demanding. They just wanted the company to deliver on what it promised when they bought the product.

Quality, Part Two

The second part of quality from the customers' perspective was even more interesting. Customers said that quality also included "the way that the product is served or delivered." The human or emotional component turned out to be more important than the actual product.

A recent survey of customers who had left one company for another asked them why they had changed. Only a small percentage mentioned quality or price. The majority, almost 70 percent, had switched because of a "perceived *indifference* on the part of someone in the company."

Most people who stop buying from a business do so because the human element is deficient in some way. They phone in with a question or complaint and are either routed through a complicated answering and voice-mail system or left on hold for a long time.

This is quite common. A major computer manufacturer was recently castigated in the business press because the average person calling on its problem hotline was required to wait for more than 30 minutes before someone picked up the phone. Their stock value fell by billions of dollars as a result of this negative story.

Customers are very sensitive. Because of the incredible competition for their business, customers can be picky and demanding with regard to how they are treated. Customers will deal with a company only if they feel that they are appreciated and respected. They will walk away from a supplier that they have used for years if someone in that company is rude or uncaring. And they will never come back.

The Receptionist Can Kill Your Business

Not long ago I phoned a company with a need to purchase several thousand dollars of their services. The owner, a professional businesswoman, had come highly recommended.

But when I phoned, the woman who answered was one of the nastiest people I had ever spoken to. She treated me as though I had just tried to steal her purse. Her first question was a very abrupt "What do you want?"

When I said that I would like to speak with the president of the company about using her services, she said, "She's busy right now. Why don't you call back later?"

I gently but firmly insisted that I had arranged to phone her boss at this time and asked her to please tell her boss that I was on the line. When I finally got through to the president, I said, as gently as possible, "The woman who is answering your phone is not helping your business."

She laughed and said, "Oh, I know. She's got a terrible personality. Ha, ha. But you know how hard it is to get good people today. Ha, ha."

That was enough for me. I decided not to use her services and to find another supplier. I learned later that her business had gone broke. No surprise. And sadly enough, this is not all that uncommon.

We used to call our receptionist our Front Office Manager. I learned this from many excellent companies. They know that the person who answers the phone sets up the customer emotionally for

> We used to call our receptionist our Front Office Manager. I learned this from many excellent companies.

everything that happens afterwards. It all begins with the person who answers the phone. A cheerful, friendly, live receptionist makes the customer feel happy that he or she called. An impatient, bored, rude, or indifferent receptionist can turn the customer off and decide him or her immediately against doing business with this firm.

This is true of every customer contact. Everything counts. Every person with whom your customers talk and everything you do for and with your customers makes an impression, positive or negative. Nothing is neutral. The emotional element in the customers' interactions with you and your company is the fundamental ingredient of "quality" and must be managed carefully all the time.

As a frequent flier, I travel on almost every airline in America. As a result, I often find myself flying on Southwest Airlines, especially for short hops around the Southwest. It is one of my favorite airlines, not because of first-class seating and delicious meals—it offers neither—but because of its friendly people and service.

Because of its reputation for friendly service, it really surprised me when one of their flight personnel treated me with extreme rudeness on a recent trip. I noticed that this person was abrupt and rude with everyone, not just me. It was so unusual that I got his name and then wrote to the president of Southwest Airlines in Dallas. I explained how much I liked Southwest Airlines, what had happened, and how much that person's behavior had offended me.

Over the next two weeks, I got three phone calls and two letters from the president's secretary. They understood that I was expressing my displeasure only because I liked the airline so much. They were friendly and responsive. They were also appalled and distressed that one of their employees had treated one of their customers so badly.

The second time they called, they told me that they had conducted an internal review and found that this person had received complaints about his behavior in the past. They assured me that it would not happen again.

The third time they called, they asked me if they could send me a gift of appreciation for having brought this customer service problem to their attention. What an airline!

Your Company Brand

There have been many books and articles written around and about the concept of the *brand*. Tom Peters talks about the "brand called you" and how each person should strive to have a unique, personal brand that sets him or her apart from everyone else.

Products, services, and companies need brands as well. But what is a brand? In its simplest terms, a brand is a name or reputation that belongs to you.

A brand denotes a particular quality and value that customers receive when they buy your product or service that they do not receive when they buy the product or service of some other company.

The best definition of a brand is that it is composed of two elements, "The promises you *make* and the promises you *keep*."

> The best definition of a brand is that it is composed of two elements, "The promises you *make* and the promises you *keep*."

It's just like a personal reputation, which you build slowly, act by act and word by word, over the course of your lifetime. A brand is something that builds slowly and is affected by every customer contact. It usually takes many years to build a brand. Once the brand is built, you must make every effort to ensure that nothing ever happens that compromises or weakens your brand image.

Determine Your Brand

What is your brand? When people think of you or what you sell, what special *value* do they attach to your name on the product or service? What do they expect to get if they buy from you rather than from someone else? What is the special quality about what you sell that makes it different from or better than what is sold by anyone else? That is your brand.

The purpose of a business is to create and keep a customer. The true measure of business success is customer satisfaction. The key to business success is to get people to buy from you, to buy again because you treated them so well the first time, and then to tell their friends to buy from you as well.

Your *positioning*, your *reputation*, and your *brand* all combine to leave an impression in the hearts and minds of your customers. The greater clarity you have with regard to these elements, the easier it is for you to create them and then to maintain them for the long term.

The ultimate question and measure of customer satisfaction is *"Would you recommend us to others?* On a scale of one to ten, how enthusiastically would you encourage other people to buy from us, based on your experience with us and our products or services?"

As a business owner on the way to wealth, the process of branding begins with you. What is your personal brand? What could it be? What should it be in the future?

Once you have determined who you are and what you want to be known for in the future, you can then look at your company and at each product or service that you sell. What kind of a reputation do you have today? What kind of a reputation will you have in the future? What kind of a reputation should you have? What kind of a reputation could you have? What could you do, starting today, to build the kind of reputation that will cause people to buy once from you, buy again, and tell their friends?

Determine Your Future

Each of these elements is under your control. Once you have decided on the impression that you want to make and leave in the hearts and minds of your prospects and customers, you can then begin to take the necessary steps, starting now, to create that impression.

You must think about your positioning, about the words that people use to describe you, and think about how you could either improve or reinforce them. You must think about your reputation, about the way you are known to customers and non-customers, and think about how you could improve it. You must think about your brand, about the promises you make and the promises you keep, and think about how you could satisfy your customers at a higher level and with greater reliability.

Consistency Is the Key

Finally, you must organize your business so that you operate with a high level of consistency and dependability. Your customers must know that they will get what they expected every single time. Your customers must trust and believe, that in dealing with you, you will always deliver on their expectations. Once your customers come to rely on you totally for the quality of your product, and your excellent treatment of them personally, you will begin to move faster and faster along the road to wealth.

Action Exercises

1. Determine your reputation in the marketplace today. What do people say about you, your business, and your products or services when they describe you to others?

2. Decide upon the words that you want to own in your customers' minds when your name is mentioned. What could you do to ensure that these words come to mind when customers think about you?

3. Determine your quality ranking in your business or industry. On a scale of 1-10, with one being the highest, what is your score today?

4. What one action could you take or change could you make to begin improving your quality ranking by one point?

5. If your business were large, prosperous, and ideal in every way, how would people talk about it in comparison with your competitors? How would it be better than others?

6. What is your brand? What are the promises your customers expect you to keep when they buy from you?

7. If your business were rated as the best in your industry, what would be different from the way your business is today?

CHAPTER TWO

Closing the Sale

Experience is not what happens to a man; it is what a man does with what happens to him.

—Aldous Huxley

I n golf they say, "You drive for show, but you putt for dough."

In business, you manufacture, produce, market, advertise, and sell for "show," but you get paid only when you *close the sale*.

Closing the sale is the most difficult and stressful part of the sales process, both for the salesperson and for the customer. Your ability to close smoothly and professionally is absolutely essential if you want to sell more of your product or service. Fortunately, closing is a skill you can master with learning and practice.

Doubling Your Income

Many thousands of my students have doubled and even tripled their incomes by using the methods and techniques in this chapter—and so can you. The reason I am teaching you 26 sales clos-ing techniques in the pages ahead is simply this. In the average sale, over 80 percent of sales are closed after the fifth attempt at closing; this means *after* the fifth time that you have asked or given the prospect an opportunity to buy. And only about ten percent of salespeople know enough different closing tech-niques and have enough ability to ask for the sale more than five times without giving up.

Practice Makes Perfect

The more closing techniques you know, the more likely it is that you will close the sale in the course of the sales interview. Good salespeople are *made*, not born. Most of the most successful salespeople in America were at one time shy, insecure, and clumsy at selling. They became great salespeople by learning and practicing the essential skills of selling, including how to close the sale. And if you do what they do, you'll be successful too. Nothing can stop you. Now, let's begin.

First Things First

You are about to learn 26 of the most effective closing techniques ever discovered. But before we start talking about these closes, you must first master the antecedents to closing. One of Murphy's Laws is that *"before you do anything, you have to do something else first."* Before you close the sale, you have to do several other things first. Here are the two psychological antecedents to closing. You must know and use these if you want to be effective.

Believe in What You Sell

The first requirement for closing, which you've heard a thousand times, is *enthusiasm.* 51 percent of all closing effectiveness comes from your enthusiasm, your excitement about your product or service. One of the best definitions of closing is that it is a "transfer of enthusiasm." In other words, when you successfully transfer your enthusiasm about your product or service into the mind of the prospect, he or she will buy and a sale will take place.

It is essential that you have enough enthusiasm to transfer a sufficient amount into the mind of the other person. What this means is that the most effective salespeople *know* their product, *believe* in their product, and *love* their product. They are absolutely convinced that their product is valuable and important for their customer.

> **T**he most effective salespeople *know* their product, *believe* in their product, and *love* their product.

If you don't believe in your product, if you don't love your product, if you wouldn't use it yourself, or if you wouldn't sell it to your best friend or your mother, then you're probably selling the wrong product for you.

Without this deep belief in the goodness of what you're selling, you can never reach that level of enthusiasm that must be transferred into the mind of the prospect to make him or her want to buy.

By the way, I don't mean the "Rah! Rah!" jumping around type of enthusiasm. I am referring to what is called *constrained enthusiasm*. This is when your enthusiasm is pent up inside of you so that you glow with enthusiasm. You seem to have a dynamic tension, an excitement about you, but it isn't in how fast you talk or how quickly you move. It's contained within.

Constrained enthusiasm has one of the most powerful effects of all on other people, more than you can imagine. This is why Ralph Waldo Emerson said, *"Nothing great was ever accomplished without enthusiasm."*

Expect the Best

The second psychological quality you require to close the sale is an attitude of *confident expectancy*. You must confidently expect that the person is going to say "yes" if you just persist long enough and ask often enough. When you ask the prospect to buy, you must confidently expect him or her to buy.

For example, you ask expectantly, "Would you like the red one or the green one today?" In other words, you don't ask, "Are you going to take one or not?" or "Is this what you had mind?" Instead, you ask for the sale expectantly. The more confidently you expect to sell, the more likely it is that you will sell.

> **Y**ou demonstrate this conviction when you confidently expect the prospect to buy.

Confidence in selling comes from knowledge. It comes from practice. It comes from experience. It comes from believing that your product will do what you say that it will do. You demonstrate this conviction when you confidently expect the prospect to buy.

Qualifying the Prospect

In the process of selling, there are several other steps that you must take before you close the sale. The first step, of course, is *qualifying*. You cannot sell a product until you know exactly what the prospect wants and needs.

Four Questions for Qualifying

To qualify effectively, you have to find the answers to four questions:

- Does the prospect *need* what you are selling?
- Can the prospect *use* what you're selling? Many people may need a piece of high-tech equipment, but they may not be able to use it because of the skill of the people or the structure of the organization.
- Can the prospect *afford* the product?
- Does the prospect *want* the product?

Desire Comes Before Closing

Before you can close, the prospect has to have made it clear that he or she has a desire to enjoy the benefits of your product or service. Once you have qualified the prospect in all four of these categories, given your presentation, and determined that he or she wants to buy, you are ready to close the sale.

Remember: most of the sale is made in the presentation. The better organized and practiced the presentation, the more likely it is that the prospect will buy what you are selling. It is in the presentation that you make your case that this product or service is the best choice for this prospect.

Why the Close Is Difficult

The moment of closing is always difficult. There is always a moment of tension. There is always a feeling of stress on the part of the prospect. This is a form of *buyer's remorse*, in advance. Whenever a prospect reaches the point of deciding, of committing to buying, tension wells up. He or she experiences the fear of failure, the fear of making a buying mistake.

Each of us, as human beings, experiences this fear of failure. The tension in the closing moments of the sale is caused by the fear of making a mistake, the fear of buying the wrong thing, the fear of paying too much, the fear of being criticized by other people. What happens when a person feels this fear? It is very much like having a spear in the stomach. What does the prospect do as a result? He or she backs away *verbally*.

Whenever a prospect experiences this fear, he or she *retreats*. The prospect says things like "Let me think it over" or "Can you leave me some material?" or "Could you call me back next week? I have to talk it over with someone else, I have to check it out first" or "I can't afford it" and so on. These are all different ways that the prospect tells you, "I am afraid of making the wrong decision."

The Fear of Rejection

The second major stumbling block at the close is the fear of rejection. It is the fear of the prospect saying "no." Each of us, deep down inside, has a fear of being told "no," a fear of being rejected. Because of this fear, we very cleverly organize our lives in such a way that we don't put ourselves in front of people that say "no." This is why salespeople actually avoid calling on new customers, to avoid being rejected.

And by the way, if you have a problem with the word "no," you've picked a very interesting profession, because four out of five sales calls end with no's, even in the very best of times. In the finest economy, with the finest product, 80 percent of your prospects are going to say *no* when you first approach them.

One of the key requirements for success in selling is the ability to hear a *no* and to keep on selling. When the prospect says, "No, I don't think so," you must be able to ignore the remark and continue with the sales process, exactly as it he or she had said nothing.

Rejection Is Not Personal

You must realize that a "no" is not *personal*. It is not aimed at you as an individual. When a prospect says *no* to you, he or she is saying "no" only to your offering. There may be a series of reasons for the rejection, most of which you can do nothing about. Your job is to face your fear, confront your fear, do the thing you fear, and ask for the order.

Expect Sales Resistance

Sales resistance is normal and natural in every sales conversation. At the moment of making a buying decision, this fear, this uneasiness, this tension starts to build up. Your job is to move through that moment of tension as quickly and as painlessly as possible. That's what good closing techniques are for.

Just remember that closing techniques are not ways of *manipulating* other people. They are not techniques to get people to buy things they don't want, don't need, can't use, and can't afford. They are techniques to help get people past that moment of tension. The professional salesperson takes the prospect smoothly past the point of closing, making it easy for the prospect to buy. The unprofessional salesperson sits there wishing and hoping and, at the end of the presentation, he asks, "Well, what do you think?"

When you ask, "Well, what do you think?" you immediately trigger the "fight or flight" reaction. The prospect's stress and tension start to build. The heart pounds faster. The blood pressure rises. The body pumps adrenaline. Finally the prospect says, "Well, I think I'd like to think about it."

Even if he or she wants it, needs it, and can afford it, the tension is too great. This is why you must know how to ask a closing question. This tension that kills so many sales is why you must learn how to close smoothly and well. This is why you must know a series of closing techniques.

1. The Appointment Close

The first closing technique is aimed at getting appointments on the telephone. If you use a telephone to get appointments, you know how difficult and frustrating it can be. Many salespeople avoid the telephone because they've been rejected and turned down so many times. The very thought of telephoning triggers feelings of fear and frustration. As a result, they seek every other way possible to make contacts. The telephone, however, is the finest and the fastest way to get good appointments—if you know how to use it properly.

In approaching the prospect by telephone, the first thing that you say has to be something that breaks preoccupation, grabs attention, and points to the result or benefit of the product.

Develop a Telephone Script

Here is an example of a telephone prospecting script. When I sold sales training programs, I found that I could get appointments nine out of ten times with qualified prospects using this simple technique.

First, I would call up and ask the receptionist, "How many salespeople do you have at your company?" I had determined that my ideal prospect business had at least 20 salespeople.

If she confirmed that they had 20 or more salespeople, I would then ask, "Who is the person who makes the decisions regarding sales training in your company?"

She would say, "That would be Mr. Jones." I would say, "Thank you. What is his first name, please?" "Bill Jones." I would then ask, "Could I please speak to Mr. Jones?"

When I got through to him, I would say, "Hello, Mr. Jones, this is Brian Tracy with Brian Tracy International. Would you like to see a way to increase your sales by 20 percent to 30 percent over the next 12 months?"

> Your opening question should focus on what the customer receives as a benefit and what your product does to improve his or her life or work.

Your opening question should focus on what the customer receives as a benefit and what your product does to improve his or her life or work. Remember: no one cares about what your product *is*. Your customer only cares about what your product *does*.

What do sales managers think about all day long? What do they care about? What determines their incomes? Answer: Sales! And they think not only about sales, but about *increasing* sales in some way.

When you ask, "Would you like to see a way to increase your sales by 20 to 30 percent over the next 12 months?" the first question that the prospect asks should be "What is it?" If the prospect does not reply with the words, "What is it?" you need to rework your question until he or she does.

Sell Only the Appointment

When you are telephoning for an appointment, you are telephoning to sell a face-to-face meeting with the prospect, not to sell your product or service. The biggest mistake you can make on the first call is to start describing your product on the telephone. The minute you start to give details or prices, the prospect will almost always say, "No thanks, I'm not interested, I can't afford it, I don't have the time" and so on.

All you are asking for is *ten minutes* of his or her time. When the prospect asks, "What is it?" you respond by saying, "That's exactly what I want to talk to you about. I just need about ten minutes of your time and you can judge for yourself if it's what you're looking for."

If the prospect asks, "How much is it?" you say, "Mr. Prospect, if it's not exactly what you're looking for, there's no charge at all."

This is a powerful response. Get the price issue out of the way immediately: "If it's not exactly what you're looking for, it doesn't cost you anything."

Remember that good prospects are busy and hard to get to. Poor prospects are not busy and they're easy to get to. If you call up someone and ask for an appointment and the person says, "Sure, come on over anytime," you can be sure the person isn't going buy anything from you.

Refuse to Describe Your Product

If the prospect then asks, "Well, could you tell me a little about it?" I would say, "I would like to tell you about it over the phone, but I have something I have to *show* you. In ten minutes, I'll be able to show you what I've got and you can judge for yourself if it's what you're looking for."

The magic word is "show." As soon as you say the word *show*, you've sidestepped the request to describe it on the telephone.

If the prospect says, "Well, could you send me something in the mail?" I would say, "I would like to send it to you in the mail, but you know how bad the mails are. Why don't I drop it off personally some time this week? What about tomorrow afternoon?"

If the prospect is at all interested, he or she will say, "OK, why don't you drop it off personally?" and will agree to a time.

I would then ask, "Will you be there?" If the prospect says, "Yes, I'll be there," I would say, "That's great. Would 3:00 be convenient for you? I'll be in your neighborhood and I'll drop it off personally."

Remember: sales materials are to be left, not sent. You hand them to the prospect at the end of the sales conversation, not at the beginning, and not as a substitute for professional selling. If the prospect is not there when you arrive, refuse to leave anything behind. Instead, offer to return at another time.

Whenever possible, don't *mail* information. When people say, "Send me some information in the mail," what they're really saying is "Go away. I'm not interested." When you send it to them in the mail, it usually goes right into the wastebasket. If you're going to send things in the mail, it is better that you put it in the envelope, throw it in your own wastebasket, and save yourself the cost of a stamp.

You Be the Judge

Sometimes we make the mistake of thinking that when we mail information, we're actually making sales. But only *sales* are sales, not mailing out sales information that no one reads. Instead, you focus single-mindedly on getting ten minutes of the prospect's time. This is the key expression: "You be the judge."

"You decide for yourself if this is what you're looking for." You then repeat, "All I need is ten minutes of your time and you can judge for yourself." This assures the prospect that you will be there for only a short time and he or she can decide.

You assure the prospect that you will not use pressure. You will just show him or her what you've got, like a trader in a bazaar laying out wares. If the prospect is not interested within ten minutes, you assure him or her that you will leave.

I have found that if you ask for 30 minutes, you may have to wait for weeks, maybe forever. If you ask for ten minutes, you can almost always be inserted into the schedule.

Be Flexible but Firm

Don't make the mistake of using the old high-pressure sales trick of saying, "How about 10:00 today or 2:00 tomorrow?" This type of *alternative close* has been used so many times that it just insults the prospect. Instead say, "Would sometime this afternoon be convenient, or perhaps tomorrow morning?"

Sometimes the prospect says, "Why don't you call me on Monday and we'll set up an appointment?" You quickly reply by saying, "Look, I've got my calendar right here. Is your calendar handy?" Of course, the prospect is sitting at his or her desk with calendar handy. You say, "Let's set up a time right now. How about 10:00 Monday morning?"

Don't allow yourself to be put off with "Call me back on Monday." It is just another

> Don't allow yourself to be put off with "Call me back on Monday."

way of getting out of seeing you face to face. The very best customers you will ever have are the ones you are going to have to fight to see the first time. They are also the ones who buy the most. When they try to put you off, when they try to avoid you and make excuses, what they're saying is that they may be very good prospects. Someone is going to get an appointment with those prospects and sell them your product—and it might as well be you.

Be persistent, be polite, and be firm. Focus only on selling that ten-minute meeting. Say, "All I need is ten minutes of your time and you can decide for yourself."

If the prospect asks for details about your product or service, you say, "It's too involved to go into on the phone, but it'll just take ten minutes and I'll show you what I've got." Sell only that ten-minute appointment. If you cannot close on telephone appointments, you can't even get to first base.

Resolve to become very good on the telephone. If you are tense about using the phone, if you're nervous, it's because you've had frustrating experiences in the past. You will become more confident as you become more competent. And competence only comes from repeated calling and experience.

2. The Approach Close

You use this approach close right at the beginning of the sales presentation. The purpose of the approach close is to get the prospect to make a commitment to giving you a decision at the end of the presentation rather than saying afterwards, "I have to think it over."

Recognize that sales resistance is the highest at the beginning of the sales presentation. This is because we live in a commercial society. Someone is trying to sell us something hundreds of times every day. We see, hear, or are otherwise exposed to thousands of advertisements each day, in the form of radio, newspapers, television, billboards, buses, and so on. Everybody's trying to sell us something, so we have natural sales resistance, from the age of five.

There is a simple and powerful way to overcome this natural resistance at the beginning of the sales conversation. You simply say this: "Mr. Prospect, I'm not here to sell you anything right now. All I'm going to do is to show you some of the reasons why other people have bought this product and continue to buy it over the years.

"And all I ask you to do is look at the reasons why others have bought it and judge for yourself. You can then tell me, one way or another, whether or not these reasons apply to you and to your situation. Is that fair? I'll just show you why others have bought it and you just tell me whether it makes sense or not to you."

The prospect will usually agree to this proposal. What you're doing is offering him or her a deal. The deal is "I won't try to sell you, if you'll listen with an open mind to my presentation."

The prospect usually says, "OK, go ahead." You then ask key qualifying questions and make your sales presentation.

At the end of the presentation, if the prospect says, "Well, I have to think it over," you can say, "Mr. Prospect, you *promised* you'd give me an answer one way or another."

It is a simple but powerful closing technique. "You promised you'd give me an answer one way or another. And from what you've said, it seems that this product is just ideal for your situation." You can then go ahead and ask for the order.

3. The Demonstration Close

This is another closing technique that you can use, right at the beginning. It is simple and effective. And you can use this close in almost any sales situation.

You use the demonstration close to qualify the prospect with your opening words and to get a clear statement from the prospect that he or she is in a position to buy and to pay for this product.

When I used this close in selling mutual funds, I would say, "Mr. Prospect, if I could show you the very best investment you've ever seen in your life, are you in a position to put $5,000 into it right now?"

The prospect might say, "Well, I don't know. I haven't got $5,000 right now."

"If you really liked it, could you invest four?"

"Well, I don't know."

"How about three?"

"Well, yes, I could invest three thousand."

"So, if I could show you the best investment you've ever seen, you could put $3,000 into it right now?"

What you've done with this approach is to change the focus of the discussion. The discussion is no longer about whether or not the prospect listens to your presentation. The main question in the prospect's mind is "Can you demonstrate or prove that you actually have an investment or a product that is as good as you say?"

Adapt the Close to Different Products

You can use this demonstration close with many different products or services.

I used to ask, "If I can show you the best sales training system that you've ever seen, are you in a position to commit to it right now?"

If the prospect says, "Well, if it's that good, I could make a decision right now," then you go through your presentation. At the end of the presentation, the prospect can't say, "Well, I have to check with the boss. I have to talk to Harry. I have to check our budget." The prospect has told you, in advance, that he or she can make the decision. The prospect has already said, in effect, "Yes, I have the money. Yes, I'm qualified. Yes, I have the authority to decide."

> A strong opening question that grabs attention and offers to give the prospect exactly what he or she wants is quite powerful.

For this reason, a strong opening question that grabs attention and offers to give the prospect exactly what he or she wants is quite powerful. If you phrase your question well, the only question the prospect should ask in response is "What is it?"

In real estate, for example, I've seen this close used over and over again. "If I could show you exactly the home you're looking for, are you in a position to make a decision today?"

One of the first questions that you should ask people when you take them out is "If we could find the exact house you're looking for, at the right price, when would you be able to take possession?" Ask them this question as you get into the car.

They may tell you that they don't know. They may tell you that they're not in the market at all. They may be just taking up your time looking at houses because they have nothing else to do. Your time is valuable and you are entitled to ask if this prospect is really capable of buying.

4. The Hot Button Close

The hot button close is considered by many sales professionals to be the most powerful closing technique of all. The hot button close is based on the fact that 80 percent of the buying decision is determined by 20 percent of the product features and benefits.

In my experience, as much as 90 percent of the buying decision is determined by about ten percent of the product features. It is up to you to find the hot button, the key benefit of your offering that the prospect wants more than anything else from your product or service. You then push this hot button over and over again. Every time you mention the hot button, the prospect's desire for your product or service increases.

Be a Sales Detective

Good salespeople are those who question skillfully and listen carefully to the answers. They listen for what is called the Freudian slip. If you ask enough questions and give prospects enough opportunity to talk, they will tell you everything that you need to know to sell them. Their reasons for buying will just "slip out."

That's why the old saying, "Telling is not selling" is true. You are selling only when you are asking questions and giving prospects the opportunity to tell you what they're looking for, what they want, what they need, what they're concerned about, what their worries are. You are selling only when you are listening attentively.

The more you ask questions and listen, the more likely it is that the prospect will say, "This is what I'm *really* looking for." This is the key benefit. For every prospect, there is a key benefit or hot button that he or she must be assured of getting before he or she will buy. Your job is to find out what it is and then convince the prospect overwhelmingly that he or she will receive that benefit.

The Flowering Cherry Tree

One of my favorite stories is about a real estate agent who takes a couple to see a home for sale. It's an old house. It's what they call a starter home, a *pre-owned* starter home, a fixer-upper, one that requires lots of work, a handyman's special.

They pull up to the house and in the back yard there is a beautiful flowering cherry tree. The first thing the wife says is "Harry, look at that beautiful flowering cherry tree. Ever since I was a girl, I've wanted to have a house with a beautiful flowering cherry tree in the back yard."

They get out of the car and go into the house. The salesman is no dummy. He knows that the final decision will be made by the woman.

Harry, Mr. Tough Guy, immediately says, "Look at this, the steps would have to be replaced."

The salesman says, "Yes, but look at that beautiful flowering cherry tree out in the yard."

They walk into the house and Harry says, "This carpet is worn out; it would have to be replaced as well."

"Yes," the salesman says, "But from here, you can see that beautiful flowering cherry tree, Mrs. Smith."

As they walk through the house, Harry says, "Look at this living room. It needs new baseboards and lights."

"Yes, but look at the beautiful view you have of that lovely flowering tree from this room," says the salesman.

This happens with almost every room.

"The kitchen needs new plumbing."

"Yes, but you can see that beautiful flowering cherry tree out the window."

"The bedrooms are too small."

"But look at the view of that beautiful flowering cherry tree from the window."

At the end of the presentation, Mrs. Smith says, "Harry, I sure do love that beautiful flowering cherry tree."

This was the hot button. And they eventually bought the house because of that flowering cherry tree.

Keep Asking Questions

Your job is to discover the hot button and then push it over and over again. It is amazing to me that sales people will talk, talk, talk, but will not ask enough questions to find out the prospect's hot button.

The prospect will say, "I'm really interested in a house with a pool."

The salesperson will say, "Isn't this a beautiful yard?"

"Yes, but it doesn't have a pool in it."

"Here's a beautiful house; you could put a tennis court over there."

"Yes, but it doesn't have a pool."

"This house has a wonderful basement."

"Yes, but it doesn't have a pool."

The prospect keeps saying, "What I want is a pool." The prospect will tell you, if you listen closely enough, exactly what he or she has to be assured of getting in your product or service. As a professional, your job is to listen for that hot button and then build your selling efforts around it. Until you know the hot button, it is almost impossible for you to make the sale.

5. The Trial Close

The trial close is a technique that a professional salesperson uses throughout the presentation to elicit feedback and to determine what the prospect is thinking and feeling about each feature.

It is also called the *check close*. You use it to check your progress.

You present a part of your product or service offering and then you ask, "Do you like this? Is this the sort of thing you're looking for? Is this what you had in mind? Is this better than the one you have right now?"

These are all trial closes. The best thing about a trial close is that the prospect can answer "no" and it doesn't end the presentation.

> The best thing about a trial close is that the prospect can answer "no" and it doesn't end the presentation.

For example, you could ask, "Is this the sort of layout that you're looking for?" The prospect might say, "No." You can then say, "That's good to know; we have several other layouts."

You could ask, "Do you like this color?" If the prospect says, "Yes," you know you are getting closer to a sale.

If the prospect says, "No, I don't like that color," you can say, "That's all right; we have several other colors available."

Ask for Feedback

The trial or check close is like a signpost at a crossroads that tells you which way to go. Imagine that you are traveling down a road and you come to a fork. At the fork, you ask, "How do you like this? Are we on the right road?" At the next fork, you check again to make sure that the customer is still happy with what you are showing him or her.

Good salespeople use trial closes throughout the sales conversation. They never present a piece of information without confirming that they are on the right track by checking.

For example, you drive up to the front of the house. You then ask, "How do you like the outside look of this house?"

You enter the house and you ask, "What do you think about this entry hallway?" You ask, "Do you like this color scheme?" You ask, "Do you like the way this is laid out?"

Professional salespeople ask questions continually. The answers give them continuous feedback that enables them eventually to develop a clear picture of exactly what the prospect wants.

6. The "Power of Suggestion" Close

The way you use the "power of suggestion" close is by creating emotions in the prospect with words or pictures. You talk as if the prospect *already* owns the product or service you are selling.

For example, you can say, "You're really going to enjoy the way this car handles on the road. My brother has one of these cars and he just loves the way it grips the road when he corners!"

You say, "You are really going to be happy when you travel in this car this summer." Or you say, "You are really going to enjoy this holiday to Europe." Or you say, "You are going to love this tour." Or you say, "You are going to enjoy living in this neighborhood. This is one of the best neighborhoods in this part of the city."

You talk to your prospects throughout as if they had already made the decision to buy. You continually create mental pictures of what it's going to be like to use, to enjoy, to benefit, and to own the product.

As you create these emotional word pictures, their thinking changes. They put themselves into the picture. Instead of thinking, "Should I buy it or not?" they are thinking of how they're going to enjoy it. You should always be talking with your prospects as if they have already bought your product or service. This suggestive language exerts a powerful influence on their thinking and decision-making.

7. The Ascending Close

The ascending close is often called the *part by part close* or the *yes, yes, yes close*. This closing technique can be used for any product or service. It's been very popular in selling mutual funds, investments, and, at one time, encyclopedias.

Encyclopedia selling is actually a perfect example. Before a person began selling encyclopedias, he or she would have to learn the encyclopedia sales presentation. The presentation was brilliant. It was designed by a group of psychiatrists in the 1950s at the cost of a quarter of a million dollars. It was then used to sell hundreds of millions of dollars worth of encyclopedias worldwide.

The ascending close works through asking questions that the prospect can only answer with "Yes" to determine if he or she is a qualified prospect. The reason this method is so powerful is that every time you ask a question and the prospect says *yes*, his or her buying temperature, or desire to own what you're selling, rises.

You don't know how high the prospect's buying temperature is when you meet him or her for the first time. But you know that there is a certain point at which the prospect will say, "I'll take it."

If you can ask enough *yes* questions, the prospect's buying desire will finally rise to the boiling point and he or she will ask, "How do I get it? When can I start? How soon will it be available?"

The Step-by-Step Closing Method

In the encyclopedia sales presentation, the salesperson starts by knocking on the door and asking, "Hello there. Do you live here?" This is a good qualifying question. If the person who answers says, "No, I'm just visiting," there is no point in continuing or making a presentation.

If the person says, "Yes, I live here," the salesperson then says, "Well, we're doing a survey in this neighborhood and we'd like to ask for your opinion on higher education. May I ask you a couple of questions?"

If the prospect answers, "Yes," the salesperson then asks, "Do you believe in the value of higher education?" If the prospect answers, "Yes," the salesperson then asks, "Do you feel that continuous learning is helpful to someone who wants to be more successful?" The prospect answers, "Yes."

After several questions like this, the salesperson asks, "Would you be interested in accepting a free set of encyclopedias from us to put in your home?"

If the prospect says, "Yes" again, the salesperson then asks, "May I come in and explain what you get?" The prospect again says, "Yes."

There were 42 "Yes" questions in the presentation.

By the end of this presentation, the prospect has said *yes, yes, yes,* over and over, and with the final *yes,* he or she has purchased a $2,000 set of encyclopedias.

> **B**y the end of this presentation, the prospect has said *yes, yes, yes,* over and over, and with the final *yes,* he or she has purchased a $2,000 set of encyclopedias.

Get the Prospect Saying Yes from the Beginning

Any presentation can be designed so that it elicits a series of *yes* answers from a qualified prospect. I design each of my sales presentations, sometimes taking many hours, so that it fits on one page, with about seven to ten questions. Each question is phrased so that it elicits a yes answer.

Each question requires the prospect to agree. Each question becomes more specific until the final *yes* question is "Would you like to take delivery right away?" The prospect answers, "Yes!" and it's a sale.

This type of presentation takes skill to design, but it is one of the most powerful methods of selling that you can ever develop and use. If ever you find yourself saying *yes, yes, yes* in a sales presentation, you know that it's perfectly professionally designed.

8. The Invitational Close

The invitational close is simply inviting the prospect to make a buying decision. My favorite invitational close is "Why don't you give it a try?"

When you ask, "Why don't you give it a try?" you are suggesting that making the purchase decision is no big deal: it is the sort of product or service that you can try out. You could ask, "Why don't you give the car a try?" This sounds like an easy decision to make.

You are suggesting that if the prospect doesn't like it, he or she can try something else. "Why don't you give it a try?" is a subtle way of saying that he or she still has options. If you are selling services or intangibles of some kind, you can ask, "Why don't you give *us* a try?" Another version of the invitational close is "Why don't you take it?"

A real estate salesman found that his sales increased almost 40 percent using this technique. Each time he showed a house to a couple, he would ask a trial closing question like "How do you like the house?" If they said, "It seems very nice," he would then ask, "Why don't you buy it? Why don't you make an offer?"

He was amazed at how many prospects said, "Well, sure. Why not?"

Other versions of the invitational close are "How many would you like?" and "What color would you like?" and "Would you like us to get started on this right way?" and "Is this what you had in mind?" In each case, you invite the prospect to make a decision instead of just standing there at the end of the presentation.

There is the story of the salesperson who comes back to the office and says, "Boy, did I have a lot of good interviews today!" The other salesperson says, "Yeah, I didn't sell anything either."

Remember that you do not offend people by asking them to make a buying decision once they have indicated an interest in the benefits of your product or service. Don't be afraid to ask, to invite them to buy.

9. The Price Close

Salespeople often say that everybody buys everything on price. They say that price is the key thing, that everybody wants the lowest price, and so on. Have you heard these arguments before?

The fact is that, in almost every case, the price is not the major reason that anyone buys anything. Price is important only when what you are selling is identical to what everyone else is selling, like gasoline at the corner station. Whenever there is a distinct difference between what you sell and what others sell, price is not the determining factor. It is salespeople who make an issue of price.

When the prospect asks, "How much is it?" the salesperson tells him the price and the prospect immediately responds with "That's too much. I can get it cheaper somewhere else. Your competitor sells it for less."

The salesperson tries to defend the price and gets into a wrestling match with the prospect.

The salesperson says, "Well, it's X dollars."

The prospect says, "I can't afford it."

The salesperson says, "But it's worth it."

The prospect says, "I can get it cheaper somewhere else."

The salesperson says, "Yes, but it's not as good as the one we've got."

And they get into an argument that goes around in circles. The fact is that you can never win by arguing on the basis of price.

Put off the Price Discussion

The basic rule on price is that, whenever possible, price should never come up until the end of the sales presentation.

In some cases, there is no way that you can avoid giving the price upfront, especially if the price is published or written down, as in selling cars or houses. But if you are selling a product or service that is more complex, where the price varies depending on what the customer buys, price shouldn't come up until the end.

People almost always object to price, no matter what it is. Everything always costs more than people expect to pay. Did you ever hear a prospect or customer say, "Wow! That's a lot cheaper than I expected"?

Everything costs more than people expected to pay. But willingness to pay and ability to pay are two different things. Very few people are willing, but many people are able. When the price question, "How much is it?" comes up before you've had a chance to show the prospect exactly what it is that he or she is getting for the money, you counter with a question: "Mr./Ms. Prospect, is price your only concern?"

> Willingness to pay and ability to pay are two different things. Very few people are willing, but many people are able.

The prospect will almost always say, "Well, no, price isn't my only concern." You say, "That's good. Could we come back to that in a minute?"

When the prospect asks right at the beginning, "How much is it?" you can say, "Mr./Ms. Prospect, the price is the best part. I'm going to cover that in just a minute, and I think you'll be very happy about it. Could I come back to that in a couple of minutes?"

The prospect will almost always agree and let you go on with the presentation. In any case, always put off the price discussion as long as possible, until you have fully described the benefits of your product or service.

Justify the Price by Emphasizing Value

When you mention the price and the prospect says, "Wow, that's a lot of money," what he or she is really saying is this: "You haven't given me enough reasons to justify that price."

Remember that a price objection is really a price *question*. A price question is when the prospect says, "That's too expensive." What he or she is saying is "From what you've told me so far, I don't see how you can charge so much for your product or service." The prospect is asking, "Can you give me some more information?"

Remember that it is not the price but the *reasons for the price* that are most important. You say, "Mr./Ms. Prospect, it may sound like a lot of money, but let me tell you why it costs what it does—and why it is worth every penny."

You then explain the values and benefits of your product or service to the prospect that more than justify the price.

Be proud of your prices. When the prospect says things like "It costs too much" or "You charge more than your competition," you say, "Mr./Ms. Prospect, you're right. As a matter of fact, it costs $1,227 more than our closest competition. And yet we sell thousands of these every year to intelligent people like you who are equally cost-conscious. Would you like to know why?"

You then explain why people buy from you and continue to buy, even at higher prices.

Make every attempt to neutralize the price objection at the beginning. If you don't do this, it just sits there like a big orang-utan in the middle of the path between you and the sale.

10. The "Just Suppose" Close

You use the *just suppose* close when the prospect says that he can't afford what you are selling. You reply and say, "Mr./Ms. Prospect, just suppose that price is not an obstacle and that we can deal with your price concerns to your complete satisfaction. Can we do that for just a moment so that I can finish showing you what I've got?"

The prospect will usually say, "OK." By the time you get to the end of the presentation, you should have explained the value of what it is you are selling in such detail, that when you tell him the price, he will see that it makes sense.

11. The "Sudden Death" Close

The "sudden death" close is a technique you can use as an *ultimatum* with a prospect who won't say *yes* and won't say *no*. You have probably had an experience where you've made a presentation and the person or the company has not made a decision. You go back to the prospect, who says he or she needs to think about it a little more. You go back again and it's the same story: he or she still needs to think about it a bit longer. The prospect won't give you an answer, one way or the other.

After four or five visits, you realize that you're spending too much time going back to this person. He or she won't make a decision and you're losing time you could be using to call on other prospects. It is time for the "sudden death" close, which works successfully about 60 percent of the time.

Here is what you do. You fill out the sales contract with all the details, except for the signature, exactly the way you've discussed the product or service. You take it back to the prospect and you say, "Mr./Ms. Prospect, we've discussed this quite a bit now and I know this is taking up a lot of your time. It's taking up a lot of my time, as well. And either this is a good idea for you or it's not. So, one way or another, let's make a decision right now. What do you say?"

You take out the contract, put a tick mark next to the signature line, put your pen on top of the contract, slide it across the desk, and say, "If you'll just *authorize* this, we can get started right away."

You then remain completely *silent* and wait. Sometimes, the silence can go on for several minutes or even longer.

But the longer you wait quietly, without speaking, the more likely it is that the prospect will decide to buy. The greater the tension, the more likely the sale. The only pressure that you are allowed to use in a sales presentation is the pressure of the silence after you've asked the closing question. And the basic rule is this: "The one who speaks first after the closing question loses."

In 60 percent of cases, the prospect will look at you, look down at the contract, look back at you, and then finally make the buying decision and sign it. In the other 40 percent of cases, the prospect will finally say, "No" and push it back to you. In either case, the indecision is over and you can get back to calling on new prospects.

12. The "Sharp Angle" Close

You use the "sharp angle" close when the prospect wants the product but is bringing up all sorts of *smoke screen* objections. These are not serious reasons for not buying. They are just excuses for not going ahead with the sale. For example, the prospect might say, "Well, I don't know if we can afford the monthly payments."

With the "sharp angle" or *bear trap close*, you turn the objection around and use it as a reason for buying. You reply, "If we could spread the payments over a longer period and get them down, would you take it?"

You use the objection as a way of closing by answering it with a solution and then asking for the order. You close on the objection.

The prospect says, "I don't think that your product will perform to my specifications." You say, "If we can prove to you that it will, will you take it?"

The prospect says, "Well, I don't think you can get it here on time." You immediately say, "If we can get it to you on schedule, will you take it?"

This approach forces the prospect to say either, "Yes, I'll take it" or "That's not the real reason why I'm hesitating about making a buying decision." This gives you a chance to uncover exactly why the prospect is holding back from a decision.

13. The "Instant Reverse" Close

The "instant reverse" close is a technique you can use in many sales situations. It takes courage to use the first time, but once you are comfortable with it, it is very effective.

For example, let us say that a prospect says, "I can't afford it."

You immediately respond by saying, "That's exactly why you should buy it!"

The prospect will react with surprise. "What? How do you mean?"

You then say, "That's exactly why you should take it, Mr./Ms. Prospect." And then you explain how and why the prospect will benefit from paying more than he or she was expecting to pay for what you are selling. You may not even have an answer when you first say this, so you have to think of the answer very quickly—a logical answer. It doesn't have to be great. It just has to be logical.

Here is another way you can use the "instant reverse" close. You call a prospect to arrange an appointment and the person on the line says, "I'm not interested." (Have you ever heard that before?) You say, "Mr./Ms. Prospect, that's why exactly why I'm calling; I didn't think you would be interested."

The prospect will be caught off guard. "What do you mean?"

You say, "Mr./Ms. Prospect, most of our very best customers were not interested when we first contacted them. But now they've become our best customers and they recommend us to their friends."

The prospect will usually say, "Really, what is it then?"

And you say, "That's exactly what I would like to talk to you about; I just need ten minutes of your time and I have something I have to show you." You then move immediately to close on the appointment.

A prospect might say, "We don't use that in our house."

You say, "That's exactly why you should take it."

"What?"

"Well, if you keep using the same product, Mr./Ms. Prospect, you'll never have any idea of all the others that are available to you today." And then you proceed to ask for a few minutes to show the prospect how your product or service is better or more affordable than he or she might have thought.

14. The "Change Places" Close

The "change places" close is simple. You are giving a presentation and you are getting sales resistance. The prospect will not tell you the key issue, why he or she is holding back from buying what you are selling.

For every product or service that a prospect can buy, there is a key benefit that he or she wants to enjoy and there is a key issue or a *key objection* that stops him or her from buying it. Until you can discover that key objection and remove it, the prospect will not buy from you. Many of your closing techniques are ways of getting the prospect to tell you what is stopping him or her from making a decision.

Here is how you use the *change places close* in this situation.

You say, "Mr./Ms. Prospect, would you change places with me just for a second? Please put yourself in my shoes." (Prospects will do this if they are at all empathetic.)

You say, "Imagine if you were talking to someone that you really respected, and you were showing him a product or a service that was really good for him, and he wouldn't tell you why he wouldn't make a decision, one way or another. What would you do if you were in my position?"

Almost invariably the prospect will say, "Well, I'll tell you why I'm hesitating." And he or she will give you his or her reasons for hesitating, enabling you to overcome the hesitation and go on with the sale.

Or you can simply ask, "Mr./Ms. Prospect, what would you do in if you were in my position?"

To prompt for more information, you can ask, "Tell me, is it the money?"

If the prospect says, "Yes, it's the money," you can then ask, "Mr./Ms. Prospect, what would we have to do to satisfy you on that point?" or "What would we have to do to do make it work for you?" or "How far apart are we?" These are powerful closing questions.

If the prospect says, "No it's not the money," you can then ask, "Then may I ask what it is that is causing you to hesitate?"

If he or she then tells you the reason, you can ask, "What would we have to do to satisfy you on that point?"

Most people are honest. They will say, "This is what we would have to do to make a deal." And you say, "OK, let me see what I can do." And at least you're still in the game. You still have a chance to sell.

15. The Secondary Close

This is one of the most popular of all closing techniques. You use it to close on a secondary issue. Sometimes it is called the *minor point* close.

For example, imagine you are selling a car and the prospect has not yet made a decision. You ask, "By the way, will you want the standard CD player or the full surround sound system in your car?"

It doesn't really matter to you which the prospect chooses. If he or she gives you an answer, the prospect has decided to buy the car. The sound system is the minor point. Purchasing the car is the main issue.

Let us say you are selling a house. Before the prospects have even said that they are ready to buy it, you ask, "By the way, would you want to take possession on the 1st or the 15th of the month?"

The occupancy date is a minor or secondary point. Whichever date they select, they've made the decision to buy the house. In other words, you close on a minor question rather on the entire purchase decision. It is much easier for a prospect to make a decision on a minor point than on the whole offer.

You can always find a minor point to close on. You can ask, "Will that be cash or charge?" even before the prospect has decided whether to buy. "Well, I'll pay cash." The prospect has made the buying decision. How he or she pays for it is a minor issue.

16. The Alternative Close

The alternative close is based on the rule that you never offer a prospect the choice between something and nothing. Always make it a choice between one of two items. Always offer a choice between Product A or Product B.

"Which house do you like better? This one or that one?"

"Which car do you prefer? The two-door or the four-door?"

"Which type of tires would you like? The radials or the standard ones?"

Always give the prospect at least two choices. The prospect will often answer and say, "Well, I like product A better" or "I like product B better" or "I don't like either product." You can then ask why. This gives you an opportunity to continue selling. But don't ever ask, "Do you want this or not?"

If you have only one product, you can offer a choice in methods of payment: "Would you like to pay with cash or credit card?" You can offer a choice in delivery options: "Would you like us to send it out or would you like to take it with you?"

Always try to offer a *choice* of some kind, either of which leads to a sale.

17. The Preference Close

Always ask, "Which do you prefer?" This is called the *preference close.* "Which do you prefer?" Asking people which they prefer is a good way of finding out where you are in the sales presentation. This is another version of the alternative close and it is very effective in getting a buying response from a prospect.

18. The Assumption Close

The assumption close is often called the "talking past the sale" close. You simply assume that the person has decided to buy. You talk exactly as if he or she has just said, "Yes, I'll take it."

You assume the sale and ask something like "How would you like to make payment?" or "Where would you want this delivered?" or "How soon do you need it?"

For example, imagine that you have just finished your presentation for a new car. You ask, "How would you like to pay for this—our finance company or yours?"

Even before the prospect says, "Yes, I'll take it," you ask, "How would you like to pay for this?" You assume that he or she has decided to buy. You talk past the sale and you go on to wrap up the details. This assumption close is one of the most powerful closes you can learn. It only takes a little practice to master.

19. The "Take Away" Close

This close is based on the discovery that sometimes people are not even aware that they want the item until you suggest that they may not be able to get it. With the *"take away" close*, especially if the prospect is hesitating, you begin to suggest that the product or service may not be available.

Here's one example of the "take away" close. You finish the sales presentation and the prospect has not yet made a decision. You have answered all the objections. He or she starts saying something like "Well, it seems kind of expensive. I don't know if we can afford it right now."

You say, "Excuse me for a moment. We were talking about the blue one, weren't we? We've really had a run on the blue ones lately. They are very popular. Let me call the office (or the warehouse) and make sure we still have them in stock. May I use your telephone?"

The prospect suddenly becomes aware that he or she might not be able to get it. "Yes. You can use my telephone." At that moment, he or she has made the decision to buy. You can phone, confirm availability, and then hang up and say, "You're in luck. There's only one left and I reserved it for you."

Many people don't realize how badly they want something until you suggest to them that they can't have it. When we were teenagers, we called this "playing hard to get." You didn't even know that you were interested in that boy or girl until he or she began playing this game with you.

Retail Selling Strategy

They use this technique in retail stores all the time. You are looking at an item and the salesperson says, "Do you like that?" You say, "Yes, it looks all right." The salesperson immediately says, "Well, let me make sure we have it in your size. I'll go and check." You say, "Yes, make sure you have it in my size." Without realizing it, you have just decided to buy it.

The salesperson returns and says, "Yes, we do have it in your size; there's only one left." And suddenly you want it, before someone else gets it. This is a common closing technique in fashion sales of all kinds. Be alert when someone tries it on you.

Here is another example you may be familiar with. A woman is in a store trying on an article of clothing that's expensive. (This technique is never used with anything cheap.) At that moment, the sales clerk sends out a secret signal to other clerks. The clerk raises a hand or whatever that causes all the others to come running over.

The sales clerks cluster around the customer like hens. Almost in unison, they say, "Ooh, that looks really good on you!" And she says, "Really? You really think so?" And they say, "Oh, yes, it's perfect for you."

As soon as the customer agrees to buy the clothes, the clerks break up and rush back to their customers. The sale has been made.

My wife has come home with the funniest-looking outfits as a result of being closed like this. But she wants to try them on for me because she's not quite sure if she made the right choice. She's not quite sure why she bought them.

She comes in and she says, "Be perfectly honest with me." And I'll say, "I don't really think it suits you." And she will say,

"But everybody in the store said it looked great on me. And there was only one left in my size."

Be very alert to this technique being used on you, or on someone you know.

20. The Puppy Dog Close

This is one of the best closing techniques of all. It is based on a familiar old story.

The kids corner the parents and say, "We want a puppy. We want a puppy. We want a puppy."

The parents, knowing what is involved in caring for a dog, say, "No! You're not getting a dog. You won't take proper care of it."

The children say, "Please, please, please just take us to the pet store and let us look at the puppies!"

Eventually the parents give in and take them to the store, but just to *look*. The pet store owners, however, are smart and experienced. They know what's going on and what the parents are thinking.

When kids fall in love with a puppy and the parents are afraid to make the wrong decision, the store owners will say, "You don't have to make a final decision like this right away. You want to be sure. Why don't you take this little puppy home and just play with it for the weekend? And if you don't like it, you can bring it back on Monday."

The kids say, "Yes, yes, yes, just for the weekend, just for the weekend!"

And the parents say, "Well, all right. Just for the weekend. Just for Sunday." Well, by Sunday night, the kids have lost interest in the dog—but the parents have fallen in love with it. As a result, they end up keeping the puppy. The sale is made.

This method really works. Any time you can give your prospect an opportunity to touch, taste, feel, smell, or use the product, you can apply the puppy dog close.

Let Them Try It Out

One of the most successful photocopier distribution companies I've ever worked with has one simple marketing and sales strategy: to "place machines." They have ten trucks and 30 salespeople. All the salespeople do is to visit prospective customers and invite them to try out their machines at no charge for a week.

Once the prospects have used the machine for a week, they get used to it. They like it. They enjoy its superior features in comparison with their older copier.

Initially they may say, "No, thank you. I'm not interested. I can't afford it." But after they have used it for a week, they become accustomed to it, enjoy the convenience of it, and decide to keep it.

Let Them Experience It

One of my friends sells motor homes—big, expensive motor homes. They sell for $50,000 and $100,000 and more. He is very successful. In good times and bad, he is one of the top motor home sales professionals in America. Here is how he uses the puppy dog close.

This salesman knows that people who buy motor homes shop around before buying. They go to every vendor of motor homes within a hundred miles. Motor home owners and purchasers are fanatics, and they know everything there is to know about motor homes. So when people come into his dealership, he meets with them and talks to them. He shows them through the motor homes. He doesn't try to close them. He establishes rapport with them. He tells them his name and he learns their names. He gives them his business card. He gets their address and phone number. He says, "We have a newsletter on motor homes, and we'll put you on the mailing list."

The next weekend, he phones them at about 10:00 or 11:00 Saturday morning. Now, where are most people at 10:00 or 11:00 Saturday morning? They're at home. He says, "I'd like to take you out for lunch. I'd like to show you something absolutely fantastic. I'll pick you up at your home at 12:00."

They are pleasantly surprised and they agree. At noon, he drives up in front of their home in a big, beautiful, $100,000 motor home. He invites them to get in and he tells them he has something neat to show them. Of course, they're a little curious. He then drives them to a beautiful park just outside his city. The park has long, sloping hills and a lake with ducks and geese swimming around. There are trees on the other side and mountains in the distance.

He makes a loop in this big motor home and stops so that his prospects can sit at the kitchen table and look out the window at this beautiful view. He then says, "Sit down over here, please."

Once they are seated, he opens up the microwave, heats up the food, takes wine out of the refrigerator, puts it in a wine bucket, pours a glass for each of them, and then lays out the food, the china, and the utensils. He sits down with them and, as they're eating, he says, "Now, isn't this exactly what you want? Isn't this nice? Wouldn't it be nice to be able to do this every single weekend?"

He then says, "We have a special on a unit just like this. You can be driving it away by tomorrow afternoon. Then you will be set for the entire summer. What do you say?"

With this technique, he gives people the chance to experience the pleasures of owning a motor home. And once they have tried it out and enjoyed the benefits, they buy it. He sells more motor homes than almost anyone else in his industry.

21. The Ben Franklin Close

The Ben Franklin close is one of the most powerful of all closing techniques for a very simple reason. This method closely parallels the way you and I think and make decisions in every area of our lives. We weigh the pros and cons. We look at the reasons *in favor of* a decision and compare them with the reasons *against* making the decision.

The Ben Franklin originates with America's first self-made millionaire. Franklin developed the habit of making his decisions by taking a piece of paper and drawing a line down the center. He would write all the reasons in favor of making the decision on one side of the paper and all the reasons opposed to the decision on the other side. He would then study the lists and make his decision.

Whenever you are selling anything complex, this is an excellent method to use. When a prospect is having difficulty making up his or her mind because of a variety of factors, you say, "Mr./Ms. Prospect, let's make this decision the way Ben Franklin used to make decisions. He became one of the richest men in America making decisions this way. This is how it works."

Take the Initiative

You say, "We take a piece of paper and draw a line down the center. Then, we write down all the reasons in favor of making this purchase decision on the left side."

Pick up the pen and pad and begin writing. You list each of the features, benefits, and advantages of your product or service, saying for each, "Remember we talked about this?" and "Remember I showed you this?" and "We talked about this" and "It does this and it does that" and "You have that and it includes this" and so on.

You write down every single advantage or benefit you can think of. You restate all the good reasons for buying your product. You should have ten or 15 points. You then ask, "Is that everything, Mr./Ms. Prospect? Can you think of anything else?"

The prospect will eventually say, "No, I think that's everything."

You then say, "OK. Now, you fill out the other side." And you hand him or her the paper and the pen. You then sit quietly and wait while the prospect tries to think of reasons not to buy.

The sharpest prospect I've ever seen couldn't think of more than two or three reasons not to buy.

You then look at his or her list, you compare it with all the reasons for buying on your side of the page, and you say, "Well, Mr./Ms. Prospect, it looks like you've made your decision."

The prospect will look at the two lists and almost invariably say, "Well, yes. I guess I have." You can then go on to wrap up the sale.

Closing a Major Sale

One of my seminar students is a professional who sells and leases commercial real estate. He told me later that he had heard about this Ben Franklin close for years but he had never used it. He thought it was too old and unsophisticated.

Then he found himself in a negotiation with a large financial institution involving the sale of a series of properties between two institutions. He had been going back and forth with these people for three weeks and they hadn't made a decision.

Finally, he said, "Why don't we use the old Benjamin Franklin decision-making method?" Since they had nothing to lose, they decided to give it a try.

The salesperson told me that he followed the method word for word from the seminar. After listing all the reasons in favor of proceeding, he turned the sheet of paper over to the vice president and said, "Now, you write the reasons opposed."

The vice president could come up with only two or three reasons.

59

The salesman then said, "Well, it looks like you've made your decision."

The vice president said, "You're right. I have. Let's go ahead with it."

The salesman made a commission of more than $50,000 on that sale. He said he was just amazed.

22. The Summary Close

The summary close is used at the end of the presentation. You say, "Now, let's just briefly go over what we've talked about." You then summarize everything that you have just discussed and explained.

You summarize the features and the benefits, one by one. You go through the entire list, right down to the last reason the prospect should buy. You then ask, "Can you think of anything else?"

The prospect will usually say "No, I think you've covered everything."

You then say, "Well, then, why don't you give it a try?" or "Why don't we get started on this right away?" or "Why don't you take it?" And you just simply close the sale.

When you summarize all the reasons for buying the product or service, one after another, you build up the maximum buying desire in the prospect. You lower his or her resistance and prepare for the closing question.

Review the Features and Benefits

For example, let's say that you're selling a home. You say, "Before you make a decision, let's look at all the features of this particular home. Well, it has this open kitchen. And it has a big backyard. And it has four bedrooms and a den. It has a double garage. It is on a quiet street, close to schools and shopping. It is well built and cared for. The price fits within your guidelines."

And so on. You can probably come up with 40 positive features if you really think about it.

Often the prospect is not fully aware how good a product or service is until the salesperson describes it perfectly. A summary close can be a powerful way to convince the prospect overwhelmingly that what you are selling is the ideal choice for him or her.

23. The Order Sheet Close

The order sheet close is used at the *beginning* of the sales process, right when the conversation begins. The first thing you do is to pull out an order sheet and write the date on it. From then on, whenever the prospect says anything about the product or service, you write it on the order sheet.

The prospect may try to stop you by saying, "Wait a minute! Don't write anything down. I'm not buying anything today. I'm just looking."

You reply, "I understand, but I have a terrible memory for detail. So I like to write everything down. And if you don't buy anything today, we'll just throw it away. OK?"

And you just keep writing on the order sheet. Eventually the prospect gets used to seeing his or her information written on your sales contract. It becomes harder and harder not to be ready to buy when the sales conversation is over.

Another way that you can use the order sheet close is to just pull out the order sheet at the end of the presentation and start filling it out.

> Assume the sale and begin completing the details. The customer has to stop you from writing to stop the sale from proceeding.

Assume the sale and begin completing the details. The customer has to stop you from writing to stop the sale from proceeding.

Then you say, "Could you give me the exact spelling of your last name for mailing purposes?" If they do so, they've made the decision to buy.

24. The Relevant Story Close

This is a powerful closing technique because we make most of our buying decisions with the *right brain*. The right brain is stimulated by stories and pictures. Whenever you can create a picture, as in the "power of suggestion" close, or whenever you can use visual sales aids, or whenever you can tell a story about your product or service, you can stimulate the prospect to buy. People may forget all the technical details of your product in ten minutes, but they will remember a story about a product or service for years.

You can use a *relevant story close* when the prospect is having trouble making a decision. You can use it in the middle of a presentation, as well. You can tell a relevant story about another prospect who was hesitating about buying this product or service and then finally decided to do it. Tell how happy that person is now because of that decision.

You can use stories especially to arouse buying desire or to answer objections. To arouse buying desire, you tell stories about your happy customers and how much they enjoy using your product or service. To answer objections, you say, "That reminds me of Sam Smith, one of our best customers. He was concerned about the price as well, but now he says that this was one of the best decisions he ever made."

> To arouse buying desire, you tell stories about your happy customers and how much they enjoy using your product or service.

25. The Door Knob Close

This is also called the *lost sale close*. It is a technique that you can use when you have almost lost the sale.

Let us say that you've made your presentation. You've given it your best shot. The prospect will not budge. He still has that one major issue, that one major objection that is holding him back. He's not telling you his objection, because he knows that, if he tells you, you are going to answer it and make the sale.

You've said everything you can think of. You've asked all the right questions. "Is it the money that you're concerned about? How far apart are we? What do we have to do to make a deal today?"

The prospect keeps saying, "No. I'm not sure. I want to think it over." But he won't tell you what it is that's stopping him from buying. You know that he can afford it and that he likes it and wants it and so on.

Finally you say, "Mr. Prospect, thank you very much for your time. I know how busy you are and I appreciate your talking to me. I'll be on my way now."

You close your briefcase, stand up, and go to the door. You put your hand on the door knob. At this moment, the prospect begins to think about what he is going to do as soon as you leave. His sales resistance drops.

You then turn around and say, "Oh, by the way, just before I go, I was wondering about something. I know that you're not going to buy anything today, but I wonder if you could help me with my sales presentation. Could you tell me, what was the *real* reason that you didn't buy today?"

Often the prospect will say, "Well, I'll tell you. The real reason was this."

At that point, you take your hand off the door knob. You go back and sit down. You set down your briefcase. You say, "Mr. Prospect, I am so glad you told me that. That's my fault. Obviously I didn't explain that part of our offering to you. May I go over that point just one more time?"

Now you have the key reason for not buying. If you can answer it effectively, you can close 50 percent and more of these "lost sales."

26. The Referral Close

The basic rule is that you should never leave a prospect or a purchaser without getting at least *two referrals*. When you've finished speaking with a prospect or a client, whether he or she buys or not, there are various ways to get referrals.

Here's an example. You say, "Ms. Prospect, I know you're not in a position to make a decision today. But could you give me the names of two or three people who you think may be able to take advantage of this offer?"

This is a form of the *alternative close*. You give her a choice between two or three referrals. A prospect will almost always pick two because it's easier. She says, "Well, yes, I can give you a couple of names."

Prospects will usually give you the first names that pop into their minds, people that they know quite well. These will be the names of friends or business associates.

You then ask, "Ms. Prospect, would you happen to have their phone numbers handy?" Prospects will usually have the phone numbers nearby. You write down the numbers.

Now that you've *closed* on the phone numbers, you ask, "Which of these prospects should I call first?" Here you are using another *alternative* close.

She might say, "Well, call Bill first." Now she has answered affirmatively to four questions in a row.

You then ask, "Ms. Prospect, would you call Bill right now and tell him that I'm coming over?"

She says, "Well, sure." She picks up the phone, calls Bill, and makes an appointment with him as you sit there.

Credibility Counts

The reason why a referral is so much more powerful than a cold call is that with a referral you have all the *credibility* of the person who is referring you. With a cold call, you start off with little or no credibility at all. And credibility, the amount that the prospect trusts you and believes you, is the critical factor in buying.

You need 100 percent credibility before the prospect will buy. If you get a referral, you start off with 90 percent credibility. It's only natural. If somebody whom you know and respect sends somebody to see you, you will treat that stranger with the same courtesy as you would treat your friend.

> **A**lways ask for referrals. Never leave a presentation, if at all possible, without at least two referrals.

Always ask for referrals. Never leave a presentation, if at all possible, without at least two referrals.

Referrals Are Like Gold

Here is another idea with regard to referrals. Go back to all of your previous customers. Call them up and ask them how they are doing. Are they happy with what they bought? Do they have any problems or questions? Is there anything that you can do for them? If possible, go and call on them in person.

I have a friend who's an excellent salesperson. Every January, right after the holidays, he calls on every customer he's got. He spends two or three weeks calling all of the people who have bought from him.

After making sure that they don't have any problems and ensuring that they're happy, he asks each one for two or three referrals. It takes him the next six months to work through all those referrals. He makes half his sales for the year without any cold calling.

Any person who's been selling for more than 90 days should be working off referrals most of the time. Referrals that people give you or that come to you as a result of good things that you've done in the marketplace are worth their weight in gold.

Maximize Throwaway Presentations

Here's a technique that helped me dramatically when I started my career. It is simply this: use throwaway presentations to develop your skills.

Whenever you're doing a presentation and you realize that the prospect is not going to buy and you know you have nothing to lose, throw the whole book at him or her. Try out every closing technique, every qualifying technique, and every objection-answering technique that you can think of.

You can really learn sales techniques only by using them face to face with prospects. When you meet a person who's not going to buy, practice your skills by using them all.

In these throwaway presentations, where you just sell away until you get thrown out, you will learn more and faster about how to close good prospects than in any other way.

The Key Quality for Closing Success

Perhaps the most important quality for sales success is *boldness.* You must learn to act boldly and to close boldly. Ask for the order with boldness and courage. Ask for the sale confidently, as if you expect the prospect to buy. Act as though it's impossible to fail. Ask the closing question like it's inconceivable that the prospect could say anything but *yes.*

Look the part. Dress and groom like a top salesperson. This gives you confidence and impresses the prospect. Speak clearly and confidently. Make sure that your voice is strong and bold when you ask. Ask as if you expect the prospect to say yes.

To close strongly and consistently, you must be *enthusiastic* about what you are doing. You must love your product. You must believe in your company. You must confidently expect to succeed.

Especially, you must persist. As Napoleon Hill said, "Persistence is to the character of man as carbon is to steel."

If you persist and you refuse to give up, you must eventually succeed greatly. If you keep on selling and asking for the sale, no matter how many times prospects tell you, "No," you will become excellent in this profession. No matter how many phone calls you make, customers you approach, or doors you knock on, no matter how many times you get turned down, if you will keep persisting and persisting and persisting, you will become one of the great salespeople of your generation.

These are the 26 best closing techniques of all time. They are vital sales tools. You have to master them through study and practice. The more tools you have in your sales toolbox, the more likely you are to make a sale. For some fields of selling, you'll need only two or three closing techniques, and you'll use those all the time. But the more sales closing techniques you know, the more competent you will become at closing, the more sales you will make, and the more successful you will be.

Action Exercises

1. Think through your entire selling process, from getting the appointment to closing the sale. How could you improve it based on what you have learned in this chapter?

2. List three sales closing techniques from those described above that you could adapt to your product or service.

3. What are three changes you could make in your sales activities to increase your credibility with your prospects?

4. List the five best features and benefits of your products or services that make them superior to those of your competitors.

5. List three ways to overcome initial sales resistance when you are attempting to get the appointment.

6. Give three ways to reply when the customer says, "I can't afford it" or otherwise shows price resistance.

7. What is the best way to reply to a prospect who says, "I want to think it over"?

CHAPTER THREE

All Business Is People Business

You can do anything you wish to do, have anything you wish to have, be anything you wish to be.

—Robert Collier

The people you attract on the road to wealth will determine your success as much as or more than any other factor. At the same time, the mistakes you make in choosing these people will hinder you and hold you back as much as or more than anything else. People are everything!

To be really successful, you need the help of *lots* of people, both inside and outside of your business. Not only do you need people who can work with you and for you, but you need people on the outside who can advise you and guide you. The greater the range of your contacts and friendships in business, the more insights, ideas, and assistance you will receive. Let us start with a key entrepreneurial skill, networking.

The Skills of Networking

Network with others. Join local business associations and attend meetings regularly. Introduce yourself to other members and ask what they do. Do not talk about your own products or services. Instead, encourage other members to sell their products and services to you.

In networking, when you meet a new person, there are some powerful questions you can ask. The first is "What sort of work do you do?"

People in business love to talk about their work. When you show a genuine interest, they will tell you in great detail what they do and how it is going. Listen intently when they speak.

The key to impressing people, by the *law of indirect effort*, is to *be impressed* by them. The key to having people find you interesting is for you to find them interesting—first.

The second question you ask, when the person slows down or stops talking about his or her business, is "And then what did you do?" or "And then what did you say?"

This will usually start the person off talking again about his business and what is happening in his or her life, business or personal.

The final question, and perhaps the best of all networking questions you can ask, is this: "What would I have to know about your business to recommend a customer to you?"

People in business think about their businesses morning, noon, and night. They think about attracting and keeping customers. They think about revenues and cash flow. They think about profits and growth. When you offer to send them a customer, they will immediately like you, want to talk to you, be interested in you, and be willing to tell you even more about what they do and the type of customers they attract.

Right after you meet someone at a business meeting and get his or her business card, drop the person a note or letter to say how happy you were to meet him or her and that you look forward to seeing him or her again at subsequent meetings. Whenever possible, include a small gift, even if it is just a poem like "Don't Quit" or "Carry On" (available at no charge at www.briantracy.com).

Best of all, do everything you can to send your new contact a customer. Think of the people you know who buy from you or your friends and associates. Is there anyone who might be a prospect for your new contact? If there is, call them both and introduce them to each other. Even if nothing comes of this introduction, your new contact will be grateful and appreciative. He or she will remember you and think about you in a very positive way.

Make No Effort to Sell

In this description of networking, you will notice that I advised against trying to sell your products or services to the people you meet. By the *Law of Indirect Effort*, the more you don't try to sell your product or service to people you meet, the more likely it is that they will become interested in learning about what you make or sell. The less you say, the greater the impression you make. The more you encourage a person to talk about his or her product or service, the more likely it is that he or she will be interested in your product or service.

Starting Off on the Road to Wealth

When you start a business, you will usually be all alone. Some of the biggest businesses in America were started on a kitchen tabletop (Amway Corporation) or in a garage (Hewlett-Packard, Apple Computer, Ford Motor Company). You will usually have to do everything yourself, from the first job in the morning to turning out the lights in the evening.

> When you start a business, you will usually be all alone.

When you start out, never be afraid to do "dog work." The most respected leaders are those who are always willing to roll up their sleeves and pitch in to help whenever they are needed. The example you set by getting in there and doing whatever is necessary is noticed by everyone.

The president of JetBlue Airways regularly works as a cabin steward on his flights, going up and down the aisles serving food and drinks and talking with the passengers. By staying "close to the customer," he maintains a deep sense for what people are thinking, saying, and feeling and continually finds ways to improve services.

When Alfred P. Sloan was president of General Motors, perhaps the most powerful single executive in the world, he would periodically disappear from Detroit for several days. No one would know where he had gone. During this time, he would get into his car and drive hundreds of miles out into the country to work as a salesman on the floor of a General Motors Automobile Dealership.

All day long, he would meet, greet, and interact with potential car buyers. He would ask them questions and listen to their concerns. He would demonstrate the latest GM models and ask for their opinions. He would make the sale or fail to make it based on the tastes, desires, wants, and needs of the potential customers. After he had received enough feedback, he would drive back to Detroit to take up his duties as president of the company.

By the time Sloan retired, he was admired and respected as one of the greatest executives of all time. He always seemed to have wonderful insights into the mind of car buyers. It was only years later that people finally figured out where he had gone on his private journeys and how it was that he was so aware of how customers thought and felt. Is this something you could do?

You will find that there is a direct relationship between the number of people in your market—customers, suppliers, competitors, and other entrepreneurs—with whom you associate and the level of your success.

The Power of the Mastermind

One vigorous conversation with two or three other entrepreneurs can give you ideas and insights into marketing and selling your products or services that you could get no other way. You should deliberately organize your time and activities to ensure interacting with other entrepreneurs and businesspeople regularly.

Napoleon Hill, the guru of success in the 20th century, interviewed and studied 500 successful businesspeople for 22 years. He found that they all had certain qualities in common. He also found that none of them had started off with these qualities and that all of these qualities were learnable. Based on his research, he published *The Law of Success* in 1928. He then elaborated his success formula in *Think and Grow Rich* in 1937.

In later years, when he was asked about what he considered to be the most important principle he had discovered in a lifetime of research among wealthy people, almost all of whom had gone from rags to great riches in one generation, he replied immediately, "the mastermind concept."

The Most Powerful Concept in History

The mastermind concept is quite simple. It has been discovered throughout history that whenever two people get together and talk in a spirit of harmony and goodwill, a third, *higher* mind is formed. Both of these people then seem to be able to tap into this higher form of intelligence that becomes available to both while they are talking.

In my seminars on Personal and Professional Development, I will often tell my audience, "Please take notes on what I am about to tell you. But don't write only the things I say. Write down the thoughts that pop into your mind while we are talking.

These thoughts will often come out of the ether and flash into your mind like a light bulb going off or like the lightning strike you see in the cartoons. This idea that comes to you, which may have nothing to do with what we are discussing in the seminar, may be the critical insight that will change your life."

Over the years, many people have come back to me and said that one idea that they got in a seminar with me changed their life and made them wealthy. This is not simply a matter of luck or random chance. Whenever people come together in a seminar to learn how to be more successful, a large third mind is created, almost like an invisible cloud floating above all of them. This collective mind or "over soul" may contain thousands of ideas and insights that then become available to everyone in the room.

When you are relaxed, positive, and happy, in company with other people who feel the same way, the mental energy of this super-conscious mind becomes active in your life. Be alert for it.

Create a Mastermind Group

Many participants in my Focal Point Advanced Coaching and Mentoring Program immediately return to their hometowns and start mastermind groups. One of my clients told me recently that, when he got back, he was so excited about the mastermind principle that he phoned four businesspeople in his community, none of whom he knew very well, and asked them if they would be interested in becoming part of a mastermind group. To his surprise, they all accepted immediately.

Their first meeting was over lunch at a nearby restaurant. He explained to them that, during a mastermind meeting, all subjects are on the table. People can talk about whatever they like. The goal is to share ideas and insights from your own experience that might be helpful to other people, in other lines of business.

After the first meeting, he was again surprised when each of the four businessmen phoned to thank him for inviting them to the meeting. They had all enjoyed it immensely and were very much looking forward to the next meeting. He told me he had been organizing these mastermind meetings, one day a week over breakfast or lunch, ever since. In less than three months, his business had doubled because of the ideas and insights he had gleaned from these positive, upbeat conversations with other businesspeople.

You can form a mastermind group in the same way. Take the initiative. Invite one or more businesspeople you know and respect to breakfast or lunch. Tell them or remind them of the mastermind concept and explain how helpful getting smart businesspeople together can be to each member of the group.

> Every businessperson knows, in his or her heart, that it's necessary to interact with other businesspeople in order to stay abreast of what is going on in his or her world.

You will get almost 100 percent agreement from the people you talk to. Every businessperson knows, in his or her heart, that it's necessary to interact with other businesspeople in order to stay abreast of what is going on in his or her world. But those people don't have the time until you call and offer to arrange a date and set it up. They will always be grateful to you for taking the initiative.

Some time ago, I was invited to join a mastermind group that met from 6:00 am to 7:00 am once a week. The organizer of the group, a successful dermatologist, had begun building this group about two years before.

The structure of the mastermind group was simple. Each week, they selected a book and enough copies were purchased for every member of the group. During that week, each person was required to read the book. At the mastermind group meeting, one person was assigned the task of reviewing the book for the group. He would explain to the group what he had found to be the most valuable ideas in the book. This would stimulate additional discussion and opinions from other people about what they had considered to be the most valuable parts of the book.

The people invited to join the group were from different occupations or businesses, so there was no competition. Over the course of two years, reading a book every week and then reviewing it every Tuesday morning from 6:00 am to 7:00 am, the incomes and revenues of the people in that mastermind group doubled and tripled. They began to emerge as the most dynamic and successful people in their fields in the community. Word of the mastermind group got out and people begged to be allowed to join. Eventually, the founder had to cap the number of participants at 15.

But with the clamor to get into the mastermind group, it occurred to a couple of the members that it was possible to have more than one mastermind group going at the same time. As a result, they formed their own mastermind groups on different mornings but with similar structures. Soon, there were mastermind groups meeting early in the morning, before work, all over the city. And all members of those mastermind groups saw their sales, revenues, and profits increase dramatically. You can do the same at any time.

Setting up a Mastermind Group

The keys to starting and running a mastermind group are simple:

1. Select only people who are positive and successful, people you like and admire and would enjoy spending time with.

2. At the mastermind meeting, you can start things off with a general question, such as "How is everything going with everybody this week?"

3. You can also structure a mastermind meeting around a specific question, e.g., "What is the best way that you have found to keep your customers coming back?"

4. As mentioned above, you can select a book, either once a week or once a month, that everyone can read and discuss. Someone would accept the responsibility for ordering the books and everyone would pay their share of the cost.

5. When you get together, you should all agree that one person will be the mastermind *leader*. This person can alternate each time. It is the job of this person to ensure that every member gets a chance to speak, that no member dominates the conversation, which can easily happen. The group leader should keep the conversation moving, keeping it positive. Each member should be open and committed to the growth and well-being of each fellow member.

You can start a mastermind group with two people. Perhaps the best mastermind of all is a husband and wife, working together in complete harmony, both positive and committed to the success of the other.

We have found that the ideal number for a mastermind group is four or five. Below that number, you are not getting the full value of the synergy of enough minds. Above that number, it becomes more difficult for each member to contribute to the group.

Remember: ideas are the keys to your future. The more ideas that you generate, from the most people, in a variety of ways, the more likely it is that you will get the right idea at the right time. And one idea is all you need to dramatically increase your speed on the road to wealth.

Finding the People You Need

When you start your business, you will have to do everything yourself. But as soon as you begin selling and delivering your products and services, you will need help. How do you decide which people you need? How do you select them, delegate to them, and supervise them? Fortunately, these questions have been asked and answered successfully millions of times.

One of the most important of all business principles is "Think on paper." Success begins with a pad of paper, a pen, and you.

Describe Every Function

Make a list of every step or function that is necessary for you to create, acquire, market, sell, deliver, get paid, and service your product. What are the steps, from beginning to end?

Instead of writing a job description, write a "function description." Each job is made up of one or more functions. For example, when someone phones your office in response to an advertisement, the functions may include answering the phone, identifying the problem or need of the customer, transferring the call to the proper person, making the sale or taking the information for a sales call, processing the order, shipping the product, collecting payment or billing for the product, accounting for the sale, arranging to replenish the inventory, reporting the sale to the business owner, and so on.

Some of these functions can be done by one person and some of these functions have to be done by two or more. When you start off, many functions will be combined into a single job. The proper performance of each of these functions will determine the efficiency and effectiveness of your entire business.

Hiring

In thinking about hiring someone to work for you, start with *yourself*. How much do you want to earn each month and each year from your business? Select an annual income goal for yourself and divide that number by 2,000, the number of hours that the average business owner works in his or her business each year. By dividing your annual income goal by 2,000, you will get your *hourly rate*.

> The rule is that you should never do work at your hourly rate that you can hire someone else to do at a *lower* hourly rate.

From now on, you use your hourly rate as a benchmark when you think about hiring other people or outsourcing specific functions to other companies. The rule is that you should never do work at your hourly rate that you can hire someone else to do at a *lower* hourly rate.

If your annual income goal is $100,000, divide by 2,000 and you have your hourly income goal of $50 per hour. At least at the beginning, the only thing that pays $50 an hour initially is *customer acquisition*. It is *prospecting, presenting,* and *closing sales.* It is finding and getting people to buy and getting them to pay in a timely fashion.

For any job, you should hire someone who will perform that function at a lower rate than you. If your desired hourly rate is $50 an hour and you can hire a receptionist or secretary to handle paperwork at $12 an hour, you should always hire a secretary or receptionist.

Getting off the Treadmill

Many business owners become overwhelmed with work, slaving away 10, 12, and 14 hours per day, seven days per week, because they insist upon performing tasks and functions that someone else could do for far less than they aspire to earn. When you use your intelligence to hire someone to perform a function for less pay than you desire to earn, you free up more and more of your time to do those things that pay your desired hourly rate and contribute the greatest value to your company.

When I started my training and development company many years ago, I did everything. I typed my own letters, did all my own bookkeeping, made all of my own appointments, and conducted all my own sales presentations. Once I had sold a seminar or training session, I would go to the hotel or meeting place and set up the chairs and organize every aspect of the meeting. I did 100 percent of the work, from beginning to end.

My first exercise in delegating or outsourcing tasks involved typing letters. I realized that I was a poor typist and I was spending too much time producing letters that were full of mistakes. (This was before computers and word processing programs.) One day, I picked up the Yellow Pages and found a professional secretary/typist who worked for a variety of independent businesspeople. From then on, I had her type all my letters for me. This freed me up to make more sales calls and generate more revenue.

When my business grew to the point where my outside secretary was typing numerous letters for me each week, I entered into an agreement to hire a secretary part of the time. I shared an office with two other independent entrepreneurs who shared a secretary. Within three months, the secretary was working full time for me alone.

As my business grew, I hired a part-time accountant/bookkeeper. She soon became a full-time employee because of the amount of business we were generating. Later I hired a salesman and then a sales manager. One by one, I replaced myself by hiring people who could do jobs at a lower hourly rate than I desired to earn. Today, I have 22 people working for me, doing jobs and performing functions that are essential to the smooth running of our business. They all work at a lower hourly rate than I do.

The Golden Triangle of Hiring

There are three key elements to consider when hiring someone for your company—results, skills, and personality. You might call this the "Golden Triangle" of hiring. Most of your problems with staff will come from a shortfall in one of these three areas.

Results

You first make a list of every *result* that you want the new person to produce. Always focus on results rather than activities. Take 100 points and allocate them over your list of desired results, divided on the basis of value. This allocation will help you decide the most important results required. By the 80/20 rule, if you have a list of ten desired results for a job, two of those tasks will be worth 80 points and the other eight tasks will be worth only 20 points.

Skills

Once you have determined exactly what you want the person to do and the results he or she is expected to produce, the second consideration in hiring is *skills*. You look for someone with a proven track record in that area. You are seeking a candidate who has already successfully demonstrated the skills necessary to achieve the results you are hiring him or her to achieve for your company.

You always hire people based on their past performance and proven results, rather than your future hopes and ambitions or theirs. Many business owners make the mistake of hiring a com-

> Many business owners make the mistake of hiring a completely inexperienced person for an important job.

pletely inexperienced person for an important job. They hire based on what the person thinks that he or she can do in the future, rather than what he or she has have already done in the past. Occasionally, this approach will be successful, but in most cases it will either fail or be a great disappointment.

The rule is that you should never hire an inexperienced person for an important job. The only real predictor of future performance is past performance. In your interview with a candidate and your follow-up work in checking references, your most important concern is whether or not the candidate has successfully mastered the job that you are hiring him or her to do for you.

Personality

The third element to look for is *personality*. In studies of many thousands of job failures, it has been found that the cause of most of them was "wrong fit." This means that the person does not have the correct personality to fit in with you and with the other people who work on your team.

One of the basic rules of human nature is that people don't change. Over time, they become even *more* of what they already are. They don't change their basic personalities, temperaments, or work habits. You should never hire a person with a personality problem with the hope or fantasy that the person is going to change once he or she starts working in your company. It simply won't happen.

I had a woman working for me some time ago who did her job extremely well. She was in charge of mailing, shipping, and delivery and was quite competent. She had only one problem. She was short-tempered and irritable and she used foul language and would snap at other members of the staff for the slightest reason.

My role and goal in my business is to achieve and maintain harmony among my people. I will not allow a negative person to work in my company. Complaining and criticizing are grounds for immediate termination. When my staff told me about the problems they were having with this woman, I sat her down privately and told her that, no matter how good she was at her job, her behavior was not acceptable at my company.

To my surprise, she replied by saying, "Look, I'm a bitch. I've always been a bitch. I have no intentions of changing. If you don't like my personality, it's your problem. I will just go somewhere else."

Her honesty and candor were refreshing. Since I did not expect her to change or to be other than who she was, I thanked her for her openness and promised to help her get another job if she would help us to train a new person. This arrangement worked perfectly. I found her a job at another company working on the loading dock with people who didn't mind if she was short-tempered and used foul language. In return, she helped us to hire and train a new person. We parted the best of friends. And she is still working successfully at the other job.

You can ensure a high level of fit with a new hire by having the person meet with at least three other people before you make a decision. Job candidates will always be at their very best when they are talking with the boss for the first time. But when they talk with potential co-workers at their level, they usually "let it all hang out." Their true personalities emerge. They reveal themselves more openly to people who might be their co-workers in the future.

The Law of Three in Hiring

Whether you are hiring your first employee or your 20th, there are ways for you to improve the process. Over the years, with considerable experience, working with and for large and small companies, I have developed the *law of three* in hiring.

Three Candidates

This law says that, once you have decided to hire for a position, you should *interview at least three candidates* for the position before you even think of selecting one of them. Even if the first candidate you interview looks outstanding, discipline yourself to interview three and, if necessary, even more.

The more candidates you interview for a job, the better perspective you will have on the kind of people who are available. The more candidates you consider, the better feeling you will have about the kind of person you actually need. The rule is that you never hire a person on the first interview, no matter how good he or she looks.

> The more candidates you interview for a job, the better perspective you will have on the kind of people who are available.

There seems to be an almost direct relationship between the *intelligence* of the candidate and his or her ability to perform on the job. As much as 72 percent of job performance can be predicted by I.Q. And one of the ways that candidates demonstrate their intelligence is by *asking questions.*

There seems to be a direct relationship between intelligence and curiosity. The more curious the candidate is about the company and the job and future prospects, the more likely he or she is to have the natural ability necessary to become a valuable asset to your business. So, listen for good questions.

Three Times

The second application of the law of three is that, once you find a person you like, interview that person at least *three times.* Some large companies will interview candidates 7, 10, and even 20 times before hiring even a receptionist. They have learned that 95 percent of success in business will be determined by the people you select to work with you. Apply the motto made famous by Caesar Augustus two thousand years ago: "Make haste slowly," especially in hiring.

Three Places

The third application of the law of three is that you interview the person you like in *three different places.* People are like chameleons. They change their behavior and appearance when you move them around from place to place. If you like a candidate when you interview him or her in your office, interview that person again in a coffee shop across the street and then again in a restaurant down the street for lunch. The more you can move a candidate around, the more different aspects of the person you will see.

Many business owners have had the experience of interviewing a candidate in their office who looks fantastic. But when they interview the candidate a second time across the street in a coffee shop, the person does not look as good. By the time they have interviewed him or her the third time, in a nearby restaurant for lunch, they begin asking themselves what they could possibly have been thinking. The person often looks dreadful by the third interview.

Three Opinions

The fourth application of the law of three is that, once you find someone you like and you have interviewed that candidate three times in three places, have him or her interviewed by *three other people*. In my office, before we hire anyone, that person is encouraged to go around the office and meet with each of our other staff members. Sometimes we hire a person as a consultant or on a daily contract basis. We encourage

> In my office, before we hire anyone, that person is encouraged to go around the office and meet with each of our other staff members.

him or her to go around and meet other people and then have coffee or go for lunch. Then the staff members and I sit down together and share our opinions of the potential new team member. If anyone in our office does not like him or her or does not feel that he or she would fit into our business, we do not hire that person.

When I started out, I wanted to be the decision maker, especially in hiring people. I soon learned that my perspective was limited. People would say almost anything to make a good impression at the first meeting. I was busy and impulsive, going on instinct, and I would often hire candidates right away. It was only when I began to stretch out the hiring process as described above that I began to make much better decisions.

In a start-up, the turnover rate is usually more than 200 percent per year. If the business starts with five people, ten people will rotate through that business, being hired and fired over each 12-month period. This is sometimes referred to as the "revolving door" phase of a new business. This is also normal and natural when a business is starting up.

But over time, with intelligent hiring practices, you can slow down this rate of turnover dramatically. Lower your turnover, increase your profits.

In my company today, which is still a small business, my employees have been working for me for an average of more than 12 years. This has not happened by accident.

Three References

The fifth application of the law of three is to interview at least *three references* given to you by the candidate. You should never, never, never hire a person without checking his or her background first. Talk with people whom they have worked for. Talk with the people whose names they offer on their resumes. Talk with anyone you can find who has had any experience with this person.

You can call up and say, "Hello, I'm Brian Tracy, with Brian Tracy International, and I am interviewing this person for this job. Is there anything that you can tell me that will help me to make a better hiring decision?"

Sometimes they will give you an answer and sometimes they will only confirm the fact that this person worked for their company during a specific time period. Because of fears of lawsuits, most employers will not comment negatively on a former employee. In this case, there is a powerful question you can ask that any previous employer can answer without fear of litigation. It is simply this: *"Based on your experience with this person, would you hire him or her back again today?"*

The answer to this question, either positive or negative, will tell you a lot. If the reference says that he or she would not hire the candidate back, that should be a *red flag* in your interviewing process. You should confront the candidate, tell exactly what happened, and ask why his or her previous employer would not rehire him or her. Listen closely to the answer. If you have any doubt or suspicion at all, refuse to hire the person.

A wise businessman I once worked for told me, *"It is always easier to get into something in business than it is to get out of it."*

The time to think carefully about hiring a person is *before* you hire, not afterwards. The difficulties and complexities of firing can be enormous and expensive.

Personnel or Placement Agencies

One way to hire people—especially clerical, accounting, or secretarial staff—is to go through a placement agency. We have used placement agencies for years, almost always with good results. The most common way that placement agencies work today is that they will find a person for you and then charge you a premium on that employee's wages for three months. For example, if a person works at $12 an hour, the placement agency will assign him or her to you and charge you $18 per hour.

This may seem high, but it is a reasonable amount. The person remains an employee of the placement agency. At any time, you can let him or her go. You just call the placement agency and tell them you no longer want that person to come to work. You have no complications and no strings attached.

At the end of three months, you can decide to keep the person on staff permanently. At this point, the placement agency lets the person go and he or she becomes an employee of your business, at a lower hourly rate. Some of our best people have come to us this way.

Two Factors for Success

There are two factors, based on many years of research, that most adequately predict whether or not new employees will be successful.

Desire

The first factor is that they really *want* the job. They say to you, "I want to work here!"

They like you. They like the company. They are excited

about the job prospects. They are positive about being able to make a valuable contribution. They are optimistic about their future with your company and the new job. They are excited about the possibility of working with you and the people in your company. This desire to have the job is one of the very best predictors of future success.

Strong Start

The second factor that has been discovered is the need to "start them off strong." When new employees begin, you set the tone and the standard for the job from then on. New hires are most impressionable in the first few days of the job. The best way to ensure that they will turn out to be excellent employees is to load them up with lots of work from the first day. From then on, they will associate working with you with working hard most of the time. Get them working and keep them busy.

> The best way to ensure that new employees will turn out to be excellent is to load them up with lots of work from the first day.

One of the greatest motivations for employees is "challenging, interesting work." People may complain about how hard they work, but in their hearts, everyone wants to be busy all day long. The busier they are, the more they enjoy their work. The busier they are, the faster the time flies. People hate to work at a job where they feel bored and uninvolved. When employees are not fully occupied all day long, they become "clock watchers." They look forward to coffee breaks, lunches, and quitting time. This is not a good situation for you to either create or allow.

When you start a new person in your company, either you or someone else must work with that person "hands on." You must specify exactly what you want him or her to do, teach him or her how to do it if necessary, and then put your new employee to work full time. People love to be busy.

Delegating and Supervising: Five Steps

The ability to delegate is one of the key result areas of management. Fortunately, it is a skill that can be learned with practice. Delegation is an art as well as a science. Effective delegation requires time, thought, and careful consideration. It is something that you must learn to do if you want to leverage yourself to the maximum.

The first step in delegation is to become perfectly clear about the *result* that you desire from the job. The greater clarity you have with regard to the results expected, the easier it is for you to select the right person to do the job.

The second step is to select a person based on his or her demonstrated ability or success at doing this job. Never delegate an important job to a person who has never done it before. If the successful completion of the task is important to the success of your business, it is essential that you delegate it to someone who you confidently believe can complete the task satisfactorily.

Third, explain to the person exactly what you want done, the result that you expect, the time schedule that you require, and your preferred method of working. The reason that you are in a position to delegate a task is because you have probably already mastered this task. Taking the time to teach and explain the best way to do the task based on your experience is an excellent way to ensure that the task will be done as you wish and on schedule.

Step four is to set up a schedule for reporting on progress. If it is an important task, set up a deadline for completion that is a day or a week before your actual deadline. Always build some slack into the system. Then, check on the progress of the task regularly, very much like a doctor would check on the condition of a critical care patient. Leave nothing to chance.

Step five, *inspect what you expect*. Delegation is not abdication. Just because you have assigned a task to another person does not mean that you are no longer accountable. And the more important the task, the more important it is that you keep on top of it.

Managing and Motivating: Five Ingredients

Thousands of employees were interviewed about what they considered to be a "great place to work." The answers they gave were different from what the managers expected.

As mentioned above, the *first* ingredient of a good job was "challenging, interesting work." This is work that kept the employee busy and involved all day long.

The *second* ingredient was a feeling of being "in the know." A good job was defined as one where the employee felt that he or she was fully informed on what was happening in the company. The employee felt like an insider, like an important part of a larger group.

The *third* ingredient of a great place to work was a "high-trust" environment. This was defined as a job where a person could feel free to do his or her best and to make mistakes, without being criticized or fired. When employees felt that they were free to make mistakes with no punishment or hostility, they enjoyed their work much more, became more creative, and worked more effectively with other people.

The *fourth* ingredient in a good job was a caring boss and friendly co-workers. Often, the human environment was more important than anything else. People like to work in a place where they get along well with everyone. The happier they felt with their work relationships, the better they worked, the lower the level of absenteeism was, and the more productive they were.

The *fifth* ingredient for a good job turned out to be good pay and opportunities for promotion and advancement. To the surprise of many managers, the issue of pay was number five among factors that constituted a good job or a great place to work.

Money as a Motivator

Psychologists have found that a certain level of pay is essential for people to feel comfortable with their jobs, but above that level, it does not have much motivational impact. To test this idea, one company doubled the pay of all the workers and then checked to see what happened to their level of productivity. As to be expected, the productivity of the workers increased dramatically. But, to their surprise, it fell back to normal within *one hour*. After that, there was no discernable impact on work performance from the doubling of pay.

> It is only when pay is substandard or below what would normally be expected for such a job that it becomes a demotivating influence.

It is only when pay is substandard or below what would normally be expected for such a job that it becomes a demotivating influence. If companies pay too little, for any reason, their most talented people, the ones with the most skill and experience, will be the first to leave. If business owners try to save money by underpaying their staff, they will soon end up with only those people who are willing to stay and accept lower levels of pay. These are not usually the best people.

Building Your Team

One of the most important principles in management and business is *synergy*. The principle of synergy says that the output of the group is greater than the total of the individual outputs of the members of the group.

In other words, when five people work together synergistically in a team, their output and productivity can be equal to 8 or 10 or even 15 people working alone and apart as individuals. This is why your job is to maintain high levels of harmony and happiness in your workplace. When employees are positive and happy, they tend to cooperate naturally and easily and they get much more done than if there is disharmony or dissension.

The very best and most profitable companies are those that emphasize the importance of teamwork from morning to night. They think about it, talk about it, encourage it, reward it, and promote it at every opportunity. People love to be part of a larger group and to feel that they are making a real contribution to the whole company. By encouraging teamwork, you bring out the very best talents and instincts of all your people.

Five Qualities of Top Teams

Over the years, exhaustive research has been done on top teams. There seem to be five characteristics or qualities of peak-performance teams that you can incorporate into your own business. Here they are:

1. Shared goals and objectives. In a smoothly functioning team, everyone is clear about what the team is expected to accomplish. The goals of the team are shared and discussed by everyone. Each team member gives his or her ideas and input into how the goals and objectives can best be achieved. Each person feels like a part of the larger organization.

> In a smoothly functioning team, everyone is clear about what the team is expected to accomplish.

Socrates held 24 centuries ago that we learn something only by dialoging about it. What we have found is that there is a direct relationship between the amount of *discussion* people engage in about the team's goals and the amount of *commitment* they have to achieving those goals when they go back to work.

If you tell the team members what the goals of the team are and then send them back to work, they will have a low level of commitment. When they experience problems or setbacks, they will easily give up or wait for you to come around and tell them what to do.

But when you propose goals and objectives for the team and invite their input and feedback, when they go back to work they will take "ownership" of the goals and objectives. They will feel a much deeper level of commitment to achieving the goals than if they were not consulted at all.

2. Shared values and principles. In excellent teams, there is regular discussion about the values, principles, and behaviors that guide the decisions of the team. The leader encourages values such as honesty, openness, punctuality, responsibility for completing assignments, quality work, and so on. Everyone discusses and agrees on what they are.

Here's what we do in my company in a "values clarification meeting." We call a meeting and ask everyone to write down three to five values that he or she thinks should guide our company. We then go around the room and write these values on a flip chart or whiteboard. Many of the values show up on more than one list, such as "integrity, good customer service, quality work, and so on."

Once we have written all the values on a flip chart or whiteboard, we identify the ten values that appear most often on our list. We then have everyone vote for the three out of the ten that they consider to be the most important. Like an election, we count up the votes to determine the "winners." We announce the top five values that we are going to use to govern our performance and behavior in the company.

By doing it in this way, everyone has a chance to contribute. At least one of each person's ideas are included in the final tally. Once we have all agreed on the top five values, everyone feels committed to practicing those values in our business. You can conduct this exercise in about 45 minutes. You will be happily surprised at the results.

3. Shared plans of action. In this phase of team building, you go around the table and have each member of the team explain exactly what part of the work he or she is going to accept responsibility for completing. At the end of this discussion, each member knows what every other member is going to be doing and how his or her own work fits in with the work of the team.

During this discussion about individual responsibilities, each person has a chance to ask others about their job, how it will be measured, what results are expected from it, and when it must be completed. The conversation is open, honest, and free-flowing. At the end, every team member knows his or her place on the team. Every team member knows how he or she fits into the big picture. Everyone feels like a valuable part of the organization.

4. Lead the action. There must always be a clear boss or leader in any organization. Democracy is a fine concept, but it goes only so far in business. Someone must be in command and take charge. And that someone is probably *you*.

> **D**emocracy is a fine concept, but it goes only so far in business.

On a good team, everyone knows who is in charge. The leader sets an example for the others. The leader becomes the role model. If the leader expects team members to do their assignments well and complete them on time, the leader leads by example and does his or her assignments well and on time, if not in advance.

In addition, the leader of a business team has a special function—to act as a "blocker" and remove the obstacles that may hinder team members from doing their jobs. The job of the leader is to make sure each team member has the time, resources, equipment, and support necessary to do his or her job in an excellent fashion. The leader not only "leads the charge," but also makes sure that the others are free to concentrate on doing the best job they possibly can.

5. Continuous review and evaluation. In this final phase, the team regularly evaluates its progress from two perspectives.

First, is the team getting the results that are expected by its customers or others in the company? In dealing with customers, the team sets up mechanisms to continually ask customers, "How are we doing?"

The best businesses have their hands on the pulse of the customer at all times. They are continually asking their customers, in every way possible, directly and indirectly, for feedback. They are not afraid of criticism or negative responses. Top teams know that they can grow only if their customers are telling them honestly what they are doing or failing to do.

The second area for evaluation is the functioning of the team. Is every member happy with the way the team members are working together? Are some members overloaded with work and others not busy enough? Are the values that the team has agreed upon working? Is everyone satisfied?

In the best businesses, disagreements are handled openly and honestly. If someone has a problem, he or she feels free to bring it up. The leader and the team accept responsibility for addressing the concerns of each team member. Everyone feels that they are all in the same boat together.

Bringing the Team Together

One of the most important things you do in building a peak-performance organization is to hold *regular staff meetings*. Bring your people together weekly, at a fixed time, to talk, discuss, catch up on progress, learn how the company is doing, and generally share ideas, opinions, and insights.

Here is an analogy that explains the importance of meetings. If you have ever had the experience of picking up a pebble from the bed of a river or stream, you will notice that the pebble is smooth and rounded. Why is this?

It is because the flow of water over the pebbles causes the pebbles to bump together continuously. This continuous bumping of pebble against pebble knocks off all the rough surfaces and causes each of the pebbles to become smooth and round.

It is the same with building your team. There is no other way to build a smoothly functioning, harmonious team of people than by bringing them together regularly and allowing them to bump against each other in the give-and-take of open conversation.

Running Your Staff Meeting

Once a week, ideally on Monday morning, you should bring your team together for a general discussion. Prepare an agenda that lists each member's name as an agenda item. This is to ensure that each gets a chance to talk and explain what he or she is doing and ask questions of the others.

You can start off the meeting with a brief recap of the past week. An excellent way to begin each staff meeting is with a piece of good news. It is also a good way to start off the week. You can then go around and ask each person to share with the others what he or she is doing, what his or her plans are for the week, and what questions he or she might have that can be answered at the staff meeting.

Once you have conducted the staff meeting yourself a couple of times, you can then choose one person every week to lead it. This rotation of responsibility enables staff members to grow in confidence and competence and to feel even more important and valuable to the company. And they do a surprisingly good job.

If a major subject comes up that involves only one person, offer to deal with it "off line." Arrange to meet separately with the individual affected, so as not to take up the time of the entire staff.

When you begin holding staff meetings once a week, preferably with the tables set in a square or a "U" shape, you will be amazed at the quality of ideas that come out and the harmony that develops among all the participants. It is one of the best team-building tools you will ever use.

Finding the Best People

There are a variety of ways that you can find the people that you need. Most business owners have used them all at one time or another. None of them are perfect, but as we say, "Cast a wide net."

The more ways that you have to find good people, the more probable that you will find the people you need at the right time.

1. Referrals. Fully 85 percent of key people are found through referrals and word-of-mouth. Someone knows someone who knows someone else and recommends that person to you.

> Fully 85 percent of key people are found through referrals and word-of-mouth.

The way you tap into this invisible network of possible candidates is by mentioning regularly that you are looking for good people to join your company. The word will soon get out and people will start to phone you to recommend someone who has just become available or to express interest themselves.

2. Personnel placement services. These companies continually advertise for candidates. They interview them and check their past histories and experience. They hire some and then send them on to you while keeping them on their own payroll.

You should find one or two personnel placement agencies in your community and talk with them about your present and future needs. These companies vary in quality, so you must be selective in finding a company that you are happy working with. They may charge a little more, but they can save you many hours of time-consuming interviews and frustrating experiences in employing the wrong person.

3. Newspaper advertisements. These will attract the greatest number of candidates, but you must use ads with care. You should be very clear in your ads about the results expected, the experience required, and the work responsibilities involved.

Even if you're careful and clear, nine out of ten people (or 19 out of 20) who respond to your ads will be totally *inappropriate*. It is almost as if they are applying for every job advertised in the newspaper without even reading the requirements.

If you advertise in the newspaper, create a five- to seven-part questionnaire that someone, even your receptionist, can ask of anyone who phones. A few questions about the specifics of your ad will screen callers very fast. "What sort of experience have you had in this job in the past? What company or companies have you worked for in this job? What sort of results did you get? How long have you worked in this area? What is your educational background? What kind of salary or income are you looking for?" After a few of these questions, it will be clear to both you and the caller if there's a possibility worth pursuing. If the applicant gives appropriate answers to these questions, ask for a resume, either by mail or by e-mail.

The Right Steps in Interviewing

When we advertise for a candidate, either in the newspaper or on the Internet, we ask, "Have you looked at our Web site?" This is an excellent question, because it screens out inappropriate candidates immediately.

Fully 80 percent of the people who apply for positions that we have advertised

> If a person lacks the ambition and the intelligence to check your Internet site before applying for a job, he or she simply lacks the qualifications to be successful with you.

on an *Internet* job board, who replied by *Internet*, have not even looked at our Web site. This is an immediate indication that the person is unacceptable. If a person lacks the ambition and the intelligence to check your Internet site before applying for a job, he or she simply lacks the qualifications to be successful with you.

If we like a person that we have interviewed over the phone, we send him or her to a special site to take a personality profile. The results of this personality profile are downloaded immediately to his or her Web site and to our Web site. This profile tells both the candidate and us immediately whether or not he or she has the personality we are seeking for the position.

Dehiring the Wrong People

If the front side of the coin of business is hiring the right people, the flip side of the coin is dehiring the wrong people.

The rule is "Hire slow and fire fast." If you have hired someone who is not working out, you must have the courage to let that person go. Any delay in firing an incompetent or unacceptable employee causes needless expense, stress, and demotivation among the rest of your staff.

A manager who keeps an incompetent person in place is himself or herself incompetent. The longer you keep the wrong person in the job, the worse you look to everyone around you. And every employee knows the truth about the others. Everyone knows everything.

Practice zero-based thinking with every staff member regularly. Ask yourself, "If I had not hired this person, knowing what I now know, would I hire him or her again today?"

Every person who works for you must pass that test every single day. If the person walked in and applied for his or her job today, knowing what you now know, would you hire that person? If the answer is "No," then the next question is "How do I get rid of this person and how fast?"

Firing Is an Act of Kindness

Sometimes, letting an employee go is the *kindest* thing that you can do for that person. Just because an employee is not capable of doing the job for which you have hired him or her does not mean that he or she is not capable. There are more than 100,000 different jobs in our economy and there is certainly a job somewhere for which that person is better suited. Your job is to "set that employee free" to find a job that is more appropriate for his or her talents and temperament.

Once you have decided that an employee does not have a future with your company, you must immediately make arrangements for him or her to go somewhere else.

The Termination Process

When you decide to fire an employee, you never do it in anger or with resentment. Just because a person turns out to be an imperfect employee does not mean that he or she is a bad person, just the wrong fit for that particular job.

Also, you must resist the urge to point out all the things that are wrong with the employee and how he or she has failed at the job. This simply leads to litigation and lawsuits for unfair termination.

Instead, you sit down with the employee, with the door closed and a *witness* present, and say that you have decided that it is not working out, that this is not the right job for him or her and that he or she is not the right person for this job. You tell the employee that you feel that he or she would be happier doing something else.

Interviews with terminated employees show that fully 70 percent of them have been expecting to be let go for a long time. Many of them have done everything possible to get their employers to fire them—through poor work practices, shoddy performance, lack of punctuality, and so on. Many employees have decided that they don't like their jobs, but they cannot "pull the trigger" on themselves. They need the boss to be the "bad guy" and fire them. They will continue to provoke the boss until he or she finally does it.

When you decide to let an employee go, it will seldom be a surprise to that person or anyone else. Your job is now to protect his or her self-esteem and ego at all costs. Do not attack or embarrass the employee. Simply say, calmly and firmly, that this is not the right job for him or her.

Expect Resistance and Defensiveness

Surprisingly enough, even an employee who *hates* the job and is doing poorly at it will often argue and defend himself or herself. An employee will offer or even promise to change, which you know will never happen. He or she will make excuses for problems in the past. He or she will argue and appear to be deeply offended at your decision. These reactions are very much like waves from the ocean and you are the rock. You simply let them pass over you without budging or changing your position.

You then repeat, "I hear what you are saying. But I have decided that this is not the right job for you and you are not the right person for this job. I think that you'd be happier doing something else." Repeat this statement, word for word, as often as necessary, until the employee finally accepts that his or her career with your company is finished. You can then explain what will happen next.

Decide What You Will Give Before You Fire

You are not required to give or pay a terminated employee anything. As a sign of generosity, most companies will give a terminated employee one week of pay for each year of service. This is to help the employee financially bridge to another job. Depending upon the relationship, either you can offer to phase the employee out over a few days or weeks or you can terminate the employee immediately and lead him or her to the door.

Times Change

When a business is growing and changing rapidly, employees who were ideal at one time become obsolete and no longer of use to the business. The requirements of the business have changed and responsibilities and expectations change as well. If an employee cannot continue to contribute appropriately, he or she has to go.

On one occasion, I terminated a good employee whose services were no longer required for my business. But because we had a good relationship, I allowed him to stay in the office to clear up his work. I allowed him to use our offices as a base of operations while he sought another job. He was always welcome to visit the offices and often attended company parties. This is the ideal.

In another case, the situation was so bad that I had the fired employee pack up under the close supervision of another employee, who then led that person to the door. Within one hour, I had all the locks changed, credit cards cancelled, and notices sent out that this person was no longer associated with my company. This is the worst-case scenario—but you must be prepared for it.

Always Be Cool

No matter what happens, when it comes to firing people, which will be a normal and unavoidable part of your career, you must resolve to remain calm and unruffled. Never allow yourself to become angry or to speak in a negative way about the person once he or she has gone. If necessary, you can explain to the other members of your staff that this person is no longer with the company. Do not take the low road. Explain that you had decided that the employee was no longer the right person for this job. Then, drop the subject and do not refer to the fired employee again. Focus on the future and get everyone else focused on the future as well.

The Psychology of Leadership

When you start a business, you will usually be relatively inexperienced in the cut-and-thrust of business activities. Because of your lack of experience, you will go into business with the wrong people, hire the wrong people, and get involved with the wrong people at many levels. This is normal and natural and to be expected at the beginning.

There is a universal principal called *law of attraction*. This law says, *"You always attract into your life the people, ideas, and resources in harmony with your dominant thoughts."*

The fact is that you are a living magnet. Like iron filings are attracted to a magnet, you will attract into your life the people who are in harmony with your current level of knowledge, wisdom, and experience.

The good news is that, as you grow and mature as a businessperson, you will attract into your life better and better people. You will attract better employees, better customers, better suppliers, better bankers, and better associates. But you will always get the people you deserve, based on your current level of personal and professional development.

There is another universal principle that I described in Chapter 1 called the *law of correspondence*. This law says that your outer world will tend to be a mirror image of your inner world. It says that, wherever you look, there you are.

This is another way of saying that your personal business will largely be a *reflection* of you. It will be an extension of your own personality. Whatever is going on inside of you will be reflected back to you by every aspect of your business. The people around you will always reflect your own level of maturity, experience, and character development.

The Law of the Lid

My friend John Maxwell, in his book *The 21 Irrefutable Laws of Leadership*, refers to what he calls the "Law of the Lid." He says that you are the "lid" on your business. It is your knowledge, ability, experience, and wisdom that holds down or raises up your whole business.

The more you learn and grow, the more experiences you have that you benefit from, and the wiser you become as a businessperson, the faster and more consistently your business will grow as well.

You will always attract the type of people who are in harmony with your own level of inner development. The rule is "Your life only gets better when you get better."

Your people get better only when you become a better manager. Your customers get better only when you become a better salesperson. Your business gets better only when you become a better businessperson. There are no shortcuts. And there is no other way.

Fortunately, you are in complete control of every aspect of your life. By continually reading in your field, listening to audio programs, attending seminars, and sharing ideas in your mastermind groups with other people, you become a better and better person.

As you improve on the inside, your business and every part of your life will improve on the outside. The only limits on what you can accomplish in your business are those limits you set on yourself with your thinking. You can go as fast and as far as you want on the road to wealth. It is completely up to you.

Action Exercises

1. Identify at least one business group or organization that you can join. Attend meetings regularly. Make networking with other businesspeople a regular part of your business life.

2. Take the initiative in forming a mastermind group. Call three or four other people, either in your business or in other businesses, and invite them all for lunch at a casual restaurant.

3. Write out a plan for interviewing and hiring people in the future. Like a checklist, follow it each time.

4. Determine your hourly rate and identify one or more jobs that could be done by someone who earns less than you. What kind of a person would be ideal?

5. Look for persons with successful track records doing key jobs that you have to have done. How could you attract them to work for you?

6. Conduct a values clarification exercise with your entire team. Then mutually agree to live and work by the common values.

7. Begin holding regular staff meetings to bring everyone together to talk, share, and integrate as a team. This could be one of the most important steps you take on the road to wealth.

CHAPTER FOUR

Choosing the Right Location

> There are powers inside of you, which, if you could discover and use, would make of you everything you ever dreamed or imagined you could become.
>
> —*Orison Swett Marden*

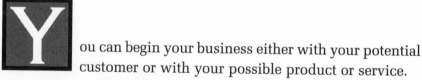 ou can begin your business either with your potential customer or with your possible product or service.

If you begin with your *customer*, you evaluate and determine what it is your customer wants, needs, and is willing to pay for that he is not yet receiving. You look for dissatisfaction in a customer's mind that you can remove. You look for a pain that you can take away. You look for a fear that you can overcome. You look for a problem that you can solve. You look for a benefit that a customer wants that he or she is not yet getting and is willing to buy and pay for if you can provide it.

If you begin with your *product or service*, you determine what it is that your product or service does to improve the life or work of your customer, and then you look out over your marketplace to find those customers for whom this is important. You think of the benefits of your product or service, your competitive advantage, your unique selling proposition, and the qualities of your product or service that make it superior to anything else that is available. You then seek out customers in the marketplace for whom these benefits are so desirable that they will buy from you rather than buy from someone else or not buy at all.

Your Place of Business

We have talked briefly about the seven parts of the marketing mix: product, price, promotion, place, packaging, positioning, and people. In this chapter, we are going to focus on your *place of business*, your geographical location where you interact with your customers and make sales.

There are many ways to "get the goods out of the woods." Most entrepreneurs start off with an idea for a single method of selling and distribution. They then stick with that method through thick and thin. No matter how many problems or difficulties they experience moving their product or service to their customers with their method or channel of distribution, they seldom consider any of the alternatives.

In this chapter, you will learn a variety of ways to get your product or service to your customer. Sometimes, changing just one method of distribution or delivery can dramatically change the entire nature of your business.

Spotting an Opportunity

When Jeff Bezos was exploring the world of Internet commerce and looking for a business opportunity, he stumbled across *books*. From time immemorial, books have been sold out of bookstores. Interested buyers go to bookstores, browse the shelves, make their selections, and pay at the cash register.

Of course, there are book clubs that enable customers to purchase books through the mail. But most book sales take place in bookstores. It had always been this way and most people believed it would always be this way.

Then Bezos came up with a big idea and a big name, "Amazon," for a big concept. He formed Amazon.com and began selling books over the Internet. This method of bookselling came together with the changing lifestyles of most book buyers to create a multibillion-dollar opportunity.

People today are busier than ever before, especially people who read and keep informed about what is going on. "One-click shopping" by Amazon enables a book buyer to go onto the Internet, find a book, order it, and get back to work in as little as one minute. No more driving halfway across town to a bookstore and spending half an hour or more browsing the shelves. The act of buying a book takes place quickly and efficiently and the book is delivered to your door in three or four days. Voilà! A billion-dollar business is born.

> "One-click shopping" by Amazon enables a book buyer to go onto the Internet, find a book, order it, and get back to work in as little as one minute.

Your Goal Is to Sell More

Your goal is to sell the very greatest amount of your products and services, at the very highest price possible, and earn the very most profit that you can from your business activities. This must be your central focus. This is your only constant. Everything else is open to change.

Most businesses find their greatest success by doing things in a different way than the founder had originally anticipated. Very often, the business owner offers a different product or service than he or she had started off producing. Sometimes he or she is selling to completely different customers and markets. Often the founder ends up selling the very most of his or her product or service in completely different ways than he or she had anticipated. And it is not uncommon for the founder to be selling different products and services to different customers and markets, using different selling and distribution channels, all at once.

The "place" is that point where your customer comes face-to-face, voice-to-voice, or ear-to-ear with your product or service and makes the decision to purchase it. Your choice of a place or location of business can make or break you. You must select it with care.

Debbi Fields' Cookies

Debbi Fields was a 20-year-old who'd grown up in Oakland, California, baking delicious cookies for her family and friends. They encouraged her to open a store and sell them to the public. Not knowing anything about retail sales, she opened a small shop, Mrs. Fields' Chocolate Chippery, in Palo Alto.

She made a variety of delicious cookies and laid them out on shelves, but no one came into her store. Too late, she realized that, because of the location of her shop, there was little or no foot traffic. People did not come to the stores in that strip mall unless they had deliberately decided to go there.

Undaunted, she took a selection of her cookies, cut them up into pieces, went down to the corner of the main street, and began offering samples to pedestrians passing by. She said, "If you like these cookies, my shop is just up the street."

This inauspicious beginning was the start of Debbi Fields' Cookies, one of the most successful businesses ever founded. Eventually, when she sold her company in 1993, it had more than 600 outlets and was doing hundreds of millions of dollars in business each year.

Debbi Fields learned her lesson from the first store. From that day forward, the company located only in stores and malls with high levels of foot traffic going past the front door. She realized that cookies are an impulse buy and the more people that are going past the store, the more people will have the impulse to walk in and buy.

Make It Easy to Buy

Human beings are *lazy* by nature. They seek comfort, convenience, and ease of purchase. Customers want to satisfy their needs in the fastest and easiest way possible. They will pay more money, and pay it faster, for a product or service that is easy to acquire, easy to use, and easy to consume. You must satisfy this need for convenience above all other things.

Not long ago, we offered a "Business Assessment Survey" on our Brian Tracy University Web site (www.briantracyu.com). The survey was free, but the software we were using required the user to complete an entire page of information in order to download the free business analysis.

We announced that this business analysis form was available at no charge to our 60,000 Entrepreneurial Newsletter subscribers. All they had to do was to come to the Web site and provide the information required and the analysis would be e-mailed to them immediately. In the first week, because of the inconvenience and complexity of the process, only about 140 entrepreneurs came to the Web site and downloaded the assessment.

We decided that this was ridiculous! We immediately rebuilt the software to make it possible for an entrepreneur to download the entire business assessment form by simply inserting his or her name and e-mail address and then pressing "submit."

We announced the availability of this form to the same group as in the previous week. This time, more than 1,400 entrepreneurs came to the site and downloaded the form, an increase of more than 1000 percent in the response rate from one minor change that made it more convenient for our subscribers.

Fish Where the Fish Are

There is a saying, "Fish where the fish are."

This means that your choice of a location or way of providing your products and services to your business has to be convenient and accessible to the greatest number of potential customers. You must carefully consider this before you make your final choice of your place of business or your main distribution channel.

> In retail business, in shopping areas, streets, or malls, the most important determinant of sales will be the number of people who walk past the front of your store.

In retail business, in shopping areas, streets, or malls, the most important determinant of sales will be the number of people who walk past the front of your store. Once people walk past the front of your store, the next determinant will be how open and inviting your store appears. How attractive does it look to a passerby? How desirable is it for a passerby who enters your store and looks around?

Store layout and design, colors and lighting, and openness and space are critical factors in creating the kind of comfort level that people need to buy a product or service from you.

The Correct Side of the Street

If you have a retail establishment that depends on people driving by your location, you must be careful about what side of the street you locate on. When I began doing real estate development, I learned to my surprise that there is both a "drive-to-work" side and a "drive-home" side of every business street or main artery.

People don't stop to shop on their way to work, only on their way home. Many beautifully designed and well-built strip shopping centers fail in the market because they are on the wrong side of the street. Many average-looking strip shopping centers are booming with business because they are on the "drive-home" side of the street. They are located in such a way that it makes it easy for the customer to buy.

Credibility Is Essential

John Paul Getty wrote a book many years ago entitled *How to Be Rich*. At that time, he was one of the richest men in the world. In the book, he advised young entrepreneurs to get an office or location on the most prestigious street in the city or town where they were located. And if possible, to get that office in one of the most prestigious buildings on the best-known street, even if it is only the size of a broom closet.

The most important word in business is "credibility." By locating on a well-known street in a well-known building, you have instant credibility. As soon as people hear about your address, they immediately grade you higher and better as a business and as a businessperson than if you were located in a suburb or on a side street.

> By locating on a well-known street in a well-known building, you have instant credibility.

Go with the Flow

There is a "small town" vs. "large city" mentality in business. What this means is that, in the main, people do not go from large cities to make their purchases in small towns, unless there are very good reasons.

In the seminar, speaking, and training business, we have found that people will come from small towns to the big city to attend a training seminar. But very few people will go from the big city to a small town for the same reason.

Whenever we work with promoters and seminar organizers, we encourage them to establish their head office in the biggest city in the state or country. In every case, without fail, where one of our representatives has decided to locate in a small town, the business has eventually failed. The majority of customers, who live in the large cities, don't take a business or a supplier located in a small town seriously. It has insufficient credibility.

Different Strokes for Different Folks

If you operate a fast-food outlet of any kind, you must be located on a high-traffic road or street. Fast food is an impulse buy. People stop to order fast food because they see the fast-food location at the same time they feel the pangs of hunger. In many cases, drivers will turn into the first fast-food outlet they see when they decide that they want to eat.

If you operate a sit-down restaurant, a drive-by location may be helpful if you are a low-cost, convenience-type sort of food, such as TGIF or California Pizza Kitchen. These outlets are dependent on drive-by traffic and ease of access for their business.

On the other hand, if you are a first-class restaurant offering high-quality, high-priced specialty foods, you can locate in an out-of-the-way place and be successful on the basis of customer satisfaction and word-of-mouth advertising. People will seek out an excellent restaurant, no matter where it is located.

If you sell your products wholesale to retail outlets or other distributors, you should locate in a business, commercial, or industrial area with ample ingress and egress for both your suppliers and your customers. You do not need special signage or drive-by visibility as a wholesale provider. Your customers are going to come to you as a result of the products that you provide and other marketing efforts.

Questions You Must Ask

There are a series of questions that you must ask and answer, over and over again, in determining where you are going to make your products and services available to the greatest number of customers. As markets and customers change their demands and preferences, you may have to revisit these questions on a regular basis.

Who Are Your Customers?

We have discussed this in an earlier chapter. The more accurately you describe your exact, ideal, perfect customer for exactly what you sell, the easier it is for you to determine your place of business or location.

Where Are Your Customers?

When we developed a shopping center recently, our major grocery store tenant insisted upon a "rooftop" survey. This is an expensive form of market analysis that determines the number of rooftops of residences within a five-mile radius of the shopping center. The major grocery stores have determined that they require 10,000 rooftops to make a grocery store economically viable. If there were fewer than 10,000 rooftops, they would put off or delay opening a business until that number of rooftops was reached.

> The major grocery stores have determined that they require 10,000 rooftops to make a grocery store economically viable.

In determining a location for a convenience store, the "rooftops" survey would be limited to homes within a one-mile radius of the prospective location. This is where the customers are. Customers will not drive more than one mile to a convenience store or more than five miles to a grocery store.

Where are *your* customers? Are they in your neighborhood? Are they in your part of the city? Are they located everywhere in your city or urban area? Are they statewide, nationwide, international?

When we conduct two- and three-day business or personal success seminars, we can predict with considerable accuracy that 80 percent to 90 percent of the participants will come from within driving distance of the seminar location. The farther away you move the seminar location, the harder it is to get people to attend the seminar because of the convenience factor.

You can also ask where your customers are located in terms of the type of businesses in which they work. Your customers could be people at certain positions at certain levels of a particular organization.

IBM changed its entire marketing strategy during the PC revolution by focusing on the purchasing managers of large companies. They determined that the decision making for computer purchases had moved from the executive suite down to the purchasing manager level. That was the location of their customers.

Another answer to "Where are my customers?" can be the geographical area in which you sell. This is often defined as your "sales territory." This is the area for which you are responsible and from which will come more than 90 percent of your customers. What is it?

When I was consulting with a *Fortune* 500 company, its large business division in San Diego had determined that there were only six potential customers for their services in the San Diego area. Each of these six major prospective customers was assigned an account manager who focused single-mindedly on getting into that company and selling products to different people at different levels of the organization. And the strategy was very successful.

When IBM started back in the 1920s, it made a decision to sell all of its products and services directly, using professionally trained salespeople. In the 1980s, with the advent of the personal computer, the customers and markets changed dramatically. At that point, IBM broke away from its traditional method of selling and began offering its products through retail stores. Why? Because customers were becoming more and more accustomed to going to retail stores to evaluate and appraise the offerings of computer companies. As a result of this shift in location, the place where it made its personal computers available, IBM increased its sales by many billions of dollars.

On the other hand, when Michael Dell began assembling computers for other students at the University of Texas in Austin, he sold his products out of his dorm room at the university. He purchased the components and assembled the computers for his friends only after they had decided what they wanted in a computer and had paid him for it.

Using this model of taking orders in advance of assembling the computer, Dell has built one of the biggest and most successful personal computer companies in the world. For years there was only one way that you could buy a Dell computer—over the phone or via the Internet. Dell Inc. chose not to offer its products through retail outlets, both to keep costs down and to keep control of the entire process.

In recent years, however, Dell has been expanding into bricks-and-mortar selling. It started small, setting up some 160 kiosks in malls and airports so potential customers could try before they buy. Then, in July 2002 it opened 21 retail outlets, but with a difference: true to Dell's direct business model, the Dell Direct Stores are mall kiosks with display models but no inventory. As of November 2005, Dell had 145 stores in 20 states, opening 61 in 2005. By mid-2006 there were more than 160 Direct Dell Stores.

Sharper Image followed a similar route. When Richard Thalheimer started The Sharper Image catalog in 1977, selling by direct mail, it was quite successful. He offered specialized products for higher-income people that were not available in most retail stores or outlets.

As The Sharper Image catalog business became more and more successful, customers began to inquire as to why The Sharper Image did not have stores in high-traffic areas so people could actually look at the products before purchasing them. These customer suggestions led Thalheimer to open a store in

1981 in San Francisco. Success there led to the development of more than 175 stores throughout the United States that have dramatically increased the sales and profitability of The Sharper Image. In 1995 The Sharper Image started selling online and within five years online sales were accounting for 15 percent of revenues. It currently has online stores in the European Union, the United Kingdom, Brazil, and Mexico.

> **A**re there different ways and places that you could offer your products for sale?

Are there different ways and places that you could offer your products for sale?

Where Do Your Customers Live?

Where do your customers work? You know that people are expedient. They prefer ease and convenience over almost anything else. They like to shop nearby.

In the first half of the century, almost all major department stores were located in downtown buildings. As the American family moved out to the suburbs, in a move that was revolutionary at that time, the major department stores, like Sears, moved out to the country as well and established large department stores in suburban malls. Today, most of the shopping in America takes place in shopping malls far away from the city center.

Is there any way that you could move your business closer to your customers to increase the ease of doing business with you?

What Are Your Customers Buying Elsewhere?

What products or services similar to yours are your potential customers buying from other sources? Could you locate your place of business where customers for what you sell go and buy from someone else?

In National City, CA, there is a stretch of National City Boulevard called "Mile of Cars." Virtually every car available in America is for sale at one of 21 dealerships on the same street. It finally dawned on all the car dealers that there would be more business for everyone if they all located close to each other and it turned out to be true. In 2000 the street running from the Interstate to "Mile of Cars" was renamed Mile of Cars Way.

When we build a shopping center, the first thing we do is to negotiate a lease with a major grocery store. Once we have the grocery store lease tied up, it is quite easy for us to rent out all the other retail space surrounding the grocery store. Hairdressers, dry cleaners, fast-food outlets, Starbucks coffee shops, gas stations, clothing stores, and even self-storage businesses want to locate where they know there is going to be a high level of consumer traffic. The spillover from this consumer traffic provides enough business for all the other stores.

What Relationships Can You Form with Other Businesses?

One of the best business strategies you can pursue is to form strategic alliances or host-beneficiary relationships with businesses that are not competing with you.

In a *strategic alliance*, you arrange with a non-competing company that is selling products and services to your ideal type of customers to sell your products as well. At the same time, you encourage your customers to buy from your ally. This is a symbiotic relationship that benefits both parties and at no cost to either.

In a *host-beneficiary relationship*, you offer something free or at a considerable discount to the customers of another company that sells a non-competing product or service to the same kind of customers that you wish to attract. In this way, it appears as though the host is giving a benefit to its customers by sending them to you for something that is free or deeply discounted.

For example, once people start to take their cars to a particular car wash, they usually return to that location over and over. To get our car wash business established in the marketplace, we visited several car dealerships and gave them coupons for free car washes to hand out to people who came to look at or buy their new cars.

It cost the host nothing to pass out these $10 gift certificates, but the customers and prospective customers greatly appreciated them. As a result, we developed a steady stream of new customers who used our car wash services once for free and then came back regularly, paying full price.

Where Do Your Customers Shop?

Human beings are creatures of habit. They get into a rhythm of shopping in a particular way, at a particular place, and then they continue to shop that way.

After you identify exactly who your customers are and exactly what they want, you can then find out where your ideal customers are currently shopping. This can lead you to either locate "where the fish are" or to advertise in that area to attract those specific shoppers to your place of business or to your products or services.

What other stores or outlets could carry your products and services as well? In other words, *where else* could you sell them? *Who else* could sell them for you? What other stores could carry your products and services along with their current lines of merchandise?

When Krispy Kreme Doughnuts was sweeping the country, one of its strategies was to not only sell from its own proprietary locations, but also through major grocery stores. This enabled the company to double the size of its sales by moving the donuts closer to greater numbers of customers and making it easier for them to buy.

Snap-on is an interesting case. It sells high-quality tools to mechanics who repair automobiles, trucks, and other vehicles. Because these mechanics are working full time, they do not have the time to go to a store to pick up the tools they need. Snap-on has therefore developed a worldwide franchise system of trucks that visit automobile and truck service and repair facilities. They bring a wide selection of tools right to the mechanics. The mechanics can then stroll out from their work bays, choose the tools that they need at this time from the Snap-on truck, and go right back to work with no loss of time. In this way, Snap-on has built a billion-dollar business.

Federal Express realized early on that it would be difficult to build a business by getting people to come to a Federal Express drop box or store to send packages. They decided to turn the overnight mail delivery business upside down. Now Federal Express sends drivers to pick up packages almost anytime, anywhere.

Of course, they still have boxes where you can drop off a Federal Express envelope for delivery by 10:30 the next morning. But if you don't have the time, you can phone Federal Express or schedule a pickup online and a driver will pick up your package within one or two hours. Federal Express now does tens of billions of dollars a year by making it easy and convenient to use its services.

Be visible to your customers. Something as simple as high-quality signage can have a major impact on your sales. If your sign is visible far enough away, you can attract passing motorists. When driving on the highway, you will often see signs that announce a restaurant or business a few miles ahead. Sometimes the sign gives the exact turnoff and directions for finding the business. They make it easy to find the business, and easy to get there.

Keep looking for ways to make it easier and more convenient to buy from you. Remember: customers are selfish, impatient, fickle, and disloyal. They will buy from whoever offers them the products and services they want, at prices they are willing to pay, the fastest and easiest way possible.

How Are You Distributing to Your Customers?

Your choice of distribution channels, of the ways that you are going to get your products and services to your customers, is one of the most important decisions you ever make. Sometimes, one small change in your place of business or the place where your customers receive your products or service can improve your sales and profitability immediately.

In my book *Getting Rich Your Own Way*, I suggested ten questions that you can ask continually to find new or better ways to distribute your products or services. Here they are once more:

1. **In what other ways could you sell your product?** Remember: there are dozens of different ways to get your products to your customers. Simply taking a product that is being sold one way and selling it in a different way can be all that it takes to start or build a successful business or to turn around an established one.

2. **What additional customers are there for your products and services?** Where are these additional customers? Who are these additional customers? Finding a new customer base for a product can be the key to making your business successful and profitable.

3. **How could you modify or change your current products or services to make them more attractive to your customers?** How could you change or improve the features or benefits you offer? Could you increase the size of the product or reduce the complexity of using it? Decrease the size or simplify the product? You must continually look for ways to offer your product or service in such a way that it is more appealing to the same or to a different customer group.

4. **What new customers could you develop for this product?** Who can you think of who can use, benefit from, and afford this product who is not buying from you or anyone else at the present? What customer groups are not using this product at all at this time? How could you appeal to these people?

5. **What new products do your customers want?** If you already have a customer base, what else do your customers need that you are not yet supplying them? What else can you offer that your customers can use in conjunction with what you are already selling them?

6. **What additional methods of distribution exist for your product?** How else could you get your product to your customers? Think of the different ways being used by other businesses. Which of them could work for you?

7. **What additional products could you distribute through your current marketing channels?** If you already have distribution channels—retail, direct selling, Internet, or direct mail—what other products could you offer that you could sell to the same customers using the same channels?

8. **What new products could you develop for your current distribution channels or your current customers?** What else could you sell through these distribution channels to these customers?

9. **What new markets exist for your new products and for your current distribution channels?** In other words, where are there people or customers who are not currently using your products or services that you could reach with your current distribution channels or methods of selling?

10. **What additional products could you produce with your current facilities?** With your current staff? With your current knowledge? With your current skills and abilities? What else could you produce? What additional products and services could you create for current markets?

Most companies and people get stuck in a comfort zone. They start off selling in a particular way, at a particular location, and ever after they continue to sell and deliver their products in the same way and the same place.

But the only real test of whether or not you are doing the right thing is sales and profitability. Are your sales high enough?

Is your business profitable enough? In what ways could you change the place and way you sell and deliver to get better results? In other words, do an opportunity gap analysis.

Selling on the Internet

Internet marketing should be a part of all your business activities. More and more people, to the tune of tens of billions of dollars each year, are buying via the Internet. It is fast, easy, convenient, and at their fingertips, anytime, anywhere. To achieve your full potential for business success, you must have an Internet presence.

There are hundreds of books written on how to sell more effectively using the Internet. But the basic truth remains the same: make it easy to buy from you!

Make your offer simple and clear. Make your prices and terms easy to understand and accept. Offer unconditional guarantees. Remove the greatest fear that Internet shoppers have, which is the fear that they will be stuck with something that is inappropriate for them. Take that fear away by giving them overwhelming guarantees and assurances of satisfaction.

Put pictures of yourself and your staff on your Web site. Give phone numbers to enable visitors to your site to contact you directly if they have a question. Develop a customer service policy for anyone who phones to request information or to purchase something from your site. Be friendly, polite, and courteous. Welcome them and thank them for calling. Thank them for their order. Make them happy that they decided to buy from you.

Keep Looking for New and Better Ways

Remember: fully 80 percent of products and services available today are new and different from what was being offered five years ago. Five years from now, 80 percent of products and services will be new and different from products and services today.

The market is developing and changing at a breakneck speed and you must move with it if you want to survive and thrive.

Read the magazines and trade journals in your field. Attend the trade shows and seminars in your industry. Read the books written by the most successful individuals and published by the most successful organizations. Keep your eyes and ears open for different ways to get your products and services to your customers. One new idea is all you need to become a major success on your way to wealth.

Action Exercises

1. Identify one way you could change your location or place of business to make it easier for people to buy from you.

2. What other channels of distribution exist for your current products or services?

3. Look around you and determine another company that is currently selling to the kind of customers who are ideal for you. How could you enter into a strategic alliance with them?

4. Seek out a business that sells to your ideal customer types and determine something that you could have that businesses give away to its customers that would bring them to you.

5. What additional products or services could you develop or offer for your current customers?

6. In what way could you improve your Internet marketing to make it easier for customers to buy from you?

7. If your business burned down today and you had to start up again in the very best location you could think of, where would it be?

CHAPTER FIVE

Proper Packaging Promotes Profits

What lies behind us and what lies before us are small matters compared to what lies within us.

—Ralph Waldo Emerson

Most people are highly visual in their orientation toward life. As much as 95 percent of the first impact you make on others with any element of your business will be what they see. That's why it is said, "You never get a second chance to make a good first impression."

When it comes to packaging, a critical element of the marketing mix, the rule is that "Everything counts!"

Everything in the visual impression that you make on your customers either helps or hurts. It either moves you toward a sale or moves you away from the sale. It either builds your credibility or reduces your credibility. It either increases the prospect's desire to buy from you or decreases it. Nothing is neutral. Everything counts!

The Effects of Buying the Wrong Product

Have you ever made a buying mistake? Have you ever bought something that turned out to be the wrong item for you and you couldn't return it? Have you ever bought something and found that you paid too much? Have you ever bought a product and then found another product that was actually better and cheaper and would have been more suitable for you? Have you ever bought something and, when you had problems, you could not return it or get it serviced? And when you phoned the company, they would not phone you back?

Have you ever bought a product or service and wished that you had never bought it at all?

If you answered *yes* to any of the above questions, join the crowd. Every person who lives in a commercial society has had hundreds, if not thousands, of bad buying experiences. When customers with bad buying experiences talk to a salesperson, enter a store, or face any situation where a purchase might take place, they become like long-tailed cats in a room full of rocking chairs. They are jumpy and nervous. They have been burned so many times before that they are determined not to have it happen again.

Here is an interesting fact about cats. If a cat sits on a hot stove, the cat will jump up and never sit on a hot stove again. But the cat will never sit on a cold stove again, either. The cat will never sit on any stove. As the saying goes, "Once burned, twice shy."

Customers are very much the same. In the experience of purchasing hundreds or even thousands of products and services over the course of a lifetime, every person has had bad buying experiences. Every person has been misled, defrauded, deceived, and cheated. Every person has purchased something and wished in retrospect that he or she had never purchased it at all.

When a customer contemplates buying from you, whatever you are selling, all of the customer's stored experiences well to the surface. The customer is automatically suspicious, skeptical, cautious, and careful. The customer is determined, consciously and unconsciously, not to be burned again.

Customers Are Seeking Reasons Not to Buy

For this reason, most customers are actually seeking reasons *not* to buy what you are selling. Even if they want what you are selling, need it, can use it to improve their lives, and can afford it, they will still be hesitant, looking around, eyes darting, seeking reasons not to buy.

> When you meet a customer for the first time, because of bad experiences his or her fear—of failure, of loss, of making a mistake—will be very high.

When you meet a customer for the first time, because of bad experiences his or her fear—of failure, of loss, of making a mistake—will be very high. And his or her belief and trust in you—your credibility—will be very low.

Changing the Balance

In my sales seminars, I illustrate this point by holding my arms straight out to my sides, with my right hand high in the air and my left hand low, like a teeter-totter with one end up and the other down. I explain to my students, "This is the equation when you meet a customer for the first time."

Referring to my right hand high in the air, I say, "This is how *high* the customer's fears and doubts about buying from you are when you first meet."

Referring to my left hand down low, I say, "This is how *low* the customer's belief and trust in you are.

"During the course of your sales conversation, you must replace the customer's natural fear and skepticism, which are very high, with a high level of confidence and belief in you and the value of your offering."

I then demonstrate that, as confidence increases, fear of making a mistake decreases. In other words, the balance changes. The customer's level of fear must eventually reach such a low point and the customer's confidence in you must reach such a high point that he or she can comfortably go ahead with the purchase.

Until this reversal occurs, like a teeter-totter going from one extreme to the other, the customer cannot and will not buy.

If the teeter-totter is equally balanced, with 50 percent fear and 50 percent confidence, the customer will just say, "Leave it with me, let me think it over."

Of course, the words "I want to think it over" really mean, "Goodbye forever!"

Throughout the world, whenever a person says, "I want to think it over," that person is actually saying, "I have decided not to buy. I am leaving now and we will never meet or speak again." There may be exceptions to this rule, but they are very rare.

The last time that you told someone that you were going to "think it over," you did not think it over at all. You forgot about that person, that product, and that company before you even got out the door or back to your car. This is the same with everyone else.

The Importance of Personal Appearance

Because customers are highly visual, the way you look on the *outside* has an enormous impact on your credibility. Your level of credibility, in turn, is the key determinant of the customer's level of fear and doubt. If you have low credibility, for any reason, the customer is left where he or she started, with high levels of fear that eliminate any possibility of buying from you, no matter what you are selling and no matter how good the price.

When I was a young salesman, coming from a poor family, I didn't know anything about dress or appearance. I wasn't afraid to work hard, cold calling, moving from office to office and door to door, being rejected over and over again, seldom making a sale.

One day, an older and wiser salesman took me aside and tentatively asked me if I was open to any advice with regard to my appearance.

I immediately felt a twinge of embarrassment. My first instinct was to reject his overture and get away. I found later that the primary reason that people do not grow and improve, in any area, is because they are afraid of feedback. Most people, from infancy and childhood, are hypersensitive to criticism and rejection.

> The primary reason that people do not grow and improve, in any area, is because they are afraid of feedback.

Even if a friend tries to offer "constructive criticism," most people don't want to hear it. Their egos are too weak, their self-image is too shallow, and their self-esteem is too low. They can't bear to hear an opinion or assessment from someone that may be a critique of some part of their appearance or behavior.

Nonetheless, I had reached the point where I believed that "It's not *who's* right but *what's* right that counts." So I said, "Sure, I would appreciate anything that you can tell me that can help me to be more effective as a salesperson."

It turned out that this salesman had started off the same way I had, coming from a poor family, wearing whatever clothes were hanging in the closet, and going out to make sales calls largely indifferent to his length of hair and his grooming. But fortunately, someone had taken him aside some years ago and given him some advice about appearance that had changed his life. He was now willing to pass the same advice onto me. It may have saved my business life.

He explained to me that 90 percent or more of the first impression that I made on a prospect would be determined by my clothes, because my clothes covered at least 90 percent of my body. Because customers were highly visual, they would be most affected by the dominant impression I made. That was my dress, from head to toe.

It turned out that my friend was an expert in men's tailoring. Over the years, I have met other people like him who have taken the time to inform themselves on proper business dress. Personally, I have read countless books and articles on subtleties and small refinements of dress that have been incredibly helpful to me.

The bottom line is this. If the first impression the customer has of you is that you are dressed poorly or improperly, for any reason, your credibility drops like a stone into a deep pool. The customer's fear of making a mistake overwhelms him or her and colors his or her thinking and emotions. The customer, even though smiling politely on the *outside*, is on the *inside* like a startled deer staring into headlamps. Poor appearance increases perceived risk. In sales, your clothes can make or break you.

The customer may be polite and friendly toward you, but because of your negative appearance, the customer has already decided that it is too risky to buy a product or service from you. In other words, referring to the customer's eyes, "The lights may still be on, but no one is home."

People do not buy products from stores or buildings. They buy products and services from *people*, from individuals with whom they are comfortable mentally and emotionally. In other words, people buy people, before they buy anything else. It is only when the customer is satisfied with his or her relationship with the salesperson that he or she seriously considers buying what is being offered.

Some time ago, I had a distributor for my training programs who was a hard worker, an ex-Marine, well educated, happily married, respected in his community, but a total *failure* in sales. He worked long hours, but he couldn't sell his way out of a paper bag. He was continually frustrated. No matter how many times he called on a prospect, and no matter how close he got to making a major sale, at the last minute the customer always decided to "think about it."

Charles came to my Advanced Selling Program, where I explained to the participants the importance of physical appearance, especially clothes and grooming. Charles stood up and demanded to know why it was that he was having such a hard time selling anything to anyone, when many other people in the room were earning hundreds of thousands of dollars a year selling the same product to very much the same type of customer.

The answer was obvious to me. Charles had a beard. He was about 30 years old and he had a full beard that came down from his sideburns and covered his full face. The hair in his beard was about one inch long, all around.

I asked him the same question, "Are you open to a little feedback about your appearance?" He was desperate by this time and willing to listen to any critique that I could give to him.

I said, "Charles, here is the result of the research. A person who wears a beard, other than an artist, a professor, or an eccentric who lives in a cabin in the woods, is assumed to have something to *hide*. A beard is like a mask, very much like the bandannas that robbers used to put over their faces when they held up the Wells Fargo stagecoach.

"This is not a conscious decision made by your customers," I told him. "It is *unconscious*. But nonetheless, when you approach a prospective customer wearing a beard, the customer automatically distrusts you. He or she may like you on the surface, but subconsciously, the customer believes that you are hiding something. You are not telling the truth. You are going to deceive him and sell him something that is either of poor quality or overpriced."

As I expected, Charles became quite irate. He said, "I have been wearing this beard since I got out of the Marines. It's part of my personality. It's one of the ways I express my individuality. Everybody who knows me expects me to have a beard. Even my wife says she likes my beard."

As gently as possible, I said, "That's all right, Charles. You can continue wearing your beard. But you should also think of going back to working for wages in a low-level job where you have little or no customer contact. You will not succeed as an entrepreneur in a competitive industry selling against other top people who look more believable than you do. You decide for yourself."

The next morning, to our surprise, Charles showed up at the training class with his beard completely shaved off. Everyone who had known him for as long as a year or two was shocked. We hardly recognized him. He looked completely different. He told us that he had worn a beard for most of his adult life. It was a surprise to him as well.

Here's the best part. The seminar took place on Friday and Saturday. On Sunday night, Charles flew back home. The next morning he went in to see a customer that he had called on several times with no success. His attitude toward Charles changed the minute he saw him. Within 30 minutes Charles made a $30,000 sale and walked out with a check for the entire amount.

He told me later that he was shocked. He had no idea that he was sabotaging his entire career, and all his hopes for his family, by wearing a beard. And what disturbed him equally as much was that no one had taken him aside to tell him about it. Everyone was afraid that he would be too sensitive.

A real estate sales manager from Phoenix told me an interesting story not long ago. He said that he had recruited a 26-year-old man, a college graduate, who had some experience in sales and wanted to get into real estate.

After this young man got his real estate license, he went out into the field, full of energy and enthusiasm, and began making multiple calls on prospective sellers of homes. After two months however, he had not listed or sold a single home.

He was thinking about giving up and doing something else. His sales manager was also thinking about encouraging him to quit and try another field. But then a friend who had been through one of my seminars told him about problems with facial hair and customers.

As it happened, this young man had grown a beard because he thought it looked "neat." He thought it was an extension of his personality that expressed his individuality. He didn't realize that prospective home sellers and buyers were turned off by his facial hair and the fact that he was young.

Fortunately, this young man was no slouch. As soon as he heard this analysis, he immediately shaved off his beard. Within two months he was the top salesman in his office. Within a year he had broken every record in his company in Phoenix. Within two years he was a superstar in the residential real estate field. He said to me later that getting rid of the beard changed his life.

"The day before I shaved my beard, people would be uninterested in talking to me. The day after I shaved my beard, I started to do more business than I ever imagined possible. It was like a miracle!"

When IBM started off, it was a largely unknown company selling data punch cards. Thomas J. Watson, the founder, realized that more than 90 percent of the impression that the company would make on prospective customers would be determined by the appearance of his salespeople.

He instituted the IBM dress code: a dark suit, a white shirt, and a dark tie. All IBM'ers wore exactly the same clothes for the next 50 years. It wasn't until the 1960s and 1970s that one of the top IBM salespeople in the country came to work with a light blue pastel shirt. There were ripples of shock throughout the organization, but his sales were so high that no one could deny that he was making a good impression on customers.

What is your company dress code? How do you dress when you deal with customers?

> What is your company dress code? How do you dress when you deal with customers?

During the dotcom boom, when many entrepreneurs were rolling in venture capital funding, they would wear flip-flops, cut-off shorts, and T-shirts to the office. Those companies had no dress codes. Everybody wore whatever they felt like, which often was what you would wear to a barbeque or picnic out in the country. But even these entrepreneurs, flaunting incorrect dress in the faces of their staff, kept suits in their offices for when customers or venture capitalists visited. Even these young people, scruffily dressed, knew that they couldn't look like bums when they were talking with people who bought their products or who supplied them with capital.

There has been a lot of talk in the last few years about "dressing down." People are encouraged to believe that they can wear whatever they feel like in the workplace. This is true, but only for one type of employee: the employee who has no future.

I wrote an article once that contained a line that was quoted over and over: "If you are a person with a future, don't dress like a person without one."

Whatever product or service you sell, you must sell it to a skeptical customer. Whatever your market, you must dress appropriately for that particular customer.

One of my clients sold grain dryers to farmers. The dress code for their salespeople was a nice pair of slacks, a sports jacket, a shirt, and a tie.

One of my client companies sells to law firms. Their dress is navy blue or grey suits or dresses, combined with low-keyed shirts and blouses, ties, and accessories. When they call on a law firm, they must look like the type of professionals that law firms are accustomed to dealing with.

Zig Ziglar says, "If you are going to give advice to people to buy your product or service, you must look like the kind of people that they are accustomed to taking advice from."

Here is a personal story. The top people within the banking industry wear gray suits. When you go to the bank to apply for a loan, it is important to wear a gray suit or skirt, blouse, or pants outfit. At an unconscious level, bankers will respond far more positively to your loan request if you look like the kind of person who is important in their world.

Once I dropped in on my banker wearing casual clothes. I had been working in my home office and was dressed in khaki pants and a golf shirt. I will never forget how negatively my banker reacted to me. He was impatient, curt, and disapproving of the loan application that I had gone there to discuss with him.

Fortunately, it was late in the day and we had to break off our conversation. We agreed to get back together again two days later. The next time we met I was dressed in a gray suit with a white shirt and a subdued tie. And I will never forget the banker's reaction. He was warm, gracious, and approving. He looked over the same loan application we had discussed two days before and approved it immediately. It was a lesson I never forgot.

In professional speaking, there is a joke question that people ask: "Do you have to be funny to be a professional speaker?" And the answer is "Only if you want you want to get paid!"

> **"Do you have to be funny to be a professional speaker?" And the answer is "Only if you want to get paid!"**

Do you have to dress in a thoughtful, credible way to sell to skeptical customers? Only if you want to get the sale!

Perhaps the most successful residential real estate company in the world is Century 21. The company started with an idea to create a national brand for local real estate agents. Instead of thousands of small real estate agencies, there would be one large, national organization that could achieve and maintain very high levels of credibility for people who wanted to buy or sell a house. And the idea worked.

Within a few years, thousands of real estate agencies were proudly flying the Century 21 banner. But because these agencies had come from so many towns and cities, with so many owners and agents, they needed something in common to bind them together.

The answer was the Century 21 gold blazer. Once they had decided on the proper design, they encouraged every Century 21 agent in the country to wear a gold blazer with prospective customers. Simultaneously, they advertised nationwide that the gold blazer was a sign of a large national company that would provide the very best services possible in buying or selling a home.

The founders and builders of Century 21 were very smart. They realized the importance of proper dress. A gold blazer is exactly the right touch in that every agent, male or female, could wear it comfortably and confidently. It had a nice look and could be tailored to the individual. People could wear a variety of pants or dresses under the blazer, but the blazer itself suggested quality, uniformity, consistency, and credibility. The results speak for themselves: Century 21 grew to be "the world's largest residential real estate sales organization, with more than 7,800 independently owned and operated franchised broker offices in over 42 countries and territories."

Read About How to Dress for Success

One of the smartest things I ever did was to begin reading books on effective dress in business. I always suggest to my audiences that they go out to their bookstore and immediately buy a book written by one of the experts on the proper clothes to wear on various business occasions.

> One of the smartest things I ever did was to begin reading books on effective dress in business.

Since they began televising debates and discussions in the U.S. Congress, almost every representative or senator has hired an image consultant so that he or she looks excellent when appearing before the cameras. You might do the same.

We could dedicate the rest of this book to the research and findings about clothing and accessories. The colors, cuts, and combinations of clothing that you wear when you deal with customers have a huge impact on whether those customers like you, trust you, believe in you, and buy your products and services.

Packaging Your Products and Services

When you think of packaging, your first thought is always the external wrappings of the product or service you sell. But unless you are selling consumer products that you ship to distant vendors, the actual packaging of the product or service comes right after the packaging of the people who sell it.

You have heard it said that "You can't tell a book by its cover."

Nonetheless, my friend Robert Ringer wrote a book that was produced by a New York publisher with a poor title and an unattractive cover. The book bombed. He bought the book back, changed the title to *Winning Through Intimidation*, changed the cover design, and sold a million copies, becoming one of the best-selling non-fiction authors in the world.

People largely make their buying decisions by the way a product or service looks on the outside.

People largely make their buying decisions by the way a product or service looks on the outside. Jan Carlzon of Scandinavian Airlines System called every customer contact a "moment of truth." It is the same with every visual impact that any part of your business makes on a customer. It is a moment of truth. It can make or break the sale. Everything counts!

Your goal must be to have first-class packaging on every product you sell. If you sell an intangible product, like consulting or financial services, everything that your customer sees or touches from your office must appear first class. It must be beautiful in every way. The customer must hold it in his or her hand and instantly conclude that whatever it contains is a high-quality item that is worth what you are asking for it.

Learn From the Best

When I started out many years ago, I had little sense for commercial art and package design. So I did the smart thing. I resolved to learn from the experts. I began reading magazines and looking at the advertisements that were the most attractive to me.

Over time, I combined the various design elements I admired into the packaging of my products and services. For example, I have always been an admirer of the IBM Corporation, having spoken for them more than 30 times. I knew that they had put a tremendous amount of time and effort into determining every single visual element in their advertising, promotion, workbooks, and manuals and in the elements of appearance that customers would see.

Research shows that *blue*, especially navy blue, expresses calmness, confidence, quality, intelligence, and value. This is why navy blue is the very best of all business colors. Whether as a suit, a blazer, a pantsuit, a dress, or even a tie, navy blue strikes people unconsciously as credible, believable, confident, and secure.

For the rest of my career, I adopted what I call "IBM Blue." Of course, I use other research-tested colors as well, like burgundy, steel gray, beige, and black, with lots of white space. But IBM Blue, combined with red or gold, is my favorite base color for letterhead, business cards, brochures, book covers, manual covers, and the outside covers of CDs, DVDs, and other products.

Use the colors that work in your industry. In each industry, there are colors that are more believable and acceptable than others. In law firms and banks, gray is a highly acceptable color. In dealing with lower-income buyers of products and services, earth tones such as brown and green are quite acceptable. Cherry red and sunshine yellow are good colors for ties and accessories. The science behind the choices and combinations of colors fill many books and libraries. You should study them.

You should think of using for packaging your products and services the same colors that are excellent on a person. The most important consideration is that people look at the packaging and immediately like the appearance and are attracted to the product or service.

Your packaging should be simple, clean, clear, bright with lots of white space, and easy to read and understand. Your packaging should inspire the reaction, "That's for me!" or "I want *that!*"

Pay Attention to Colors and Designs Around You

Walk through your local supermarket and just let your eyes wander from product to product. Whenever your eyes light on a product and you feel attracted to that product, make a note of the colors and design elements that are particular appealing.

Page through magazines and newspapers and notice the advertisements that catch your eye. Tear them out. Lay them out in front of you on a table and think about how you could combine the best elements of the ads in your package design.

> When you do design packaging for anything you sell, always ask for opinions from as many *women* as possible.

When you do design packaging for anything you sell, always ask for opinions from as many *women* as possible. Women are better buyers and shoppers than men. If something does not appeal to a woman, it will seldom appeal to a man.

Using Commercial Artists and Designers

Finding, hiring, commissioning and using commercial artists to design the visual elements of your products, services, stationery, brochures, and other elements of your business is like entering a *mine field.*

Most commercial artists started off in life with the desire to create great art, like Michelangelo or Renoir. When they found that most artists starve, they shifted gears and moved into commercial art and design in order to make a better living.

But nonetheless, many of them are haunted by the belief and hope that they could be great artists if only enough people would appreciate them. In their hearts, most commercial artists disdain the hard work of business and commerce. They look down on the petty businessperson who has to sell a product or service in an aggressive, competitive market in order to make a living.

Most commercial artists feel that they are above that sort of thing. They are too good for grubbing in the muck with the entrepreneurs. They feel that they are people of higher quality. They walk around with their noses in the air, desiring to be aloof from the businesses that hire them to design packaging and artwork.

In my experience, most commercial artists produce things that they think are "cute" or "clever" or "completely different." They are very skillful at selling businesspeople on artwork and design concepts that are completely *non-commercial.* Their designs should hang on the walls of second-rate abstract art galleries. If you put them on your products or packaging, you can destroy any desire on the part of the customer to buy from you.

My commercial artist, Camille Woodbury, has been with me for more than 15 years. She is a genius. She is brilliant at designing artwork that sells. Whether it is a book cover, a brochure, or a CD cover, she has a wonderful sense for making something look appealing to a prospective customer. Partially because of this, we have sold more than $100 million worth of our audio and video learning programs worldwide in the face of very determined competitors.

Make Your Message Clear

One of my favorite stories is about a little old lady who is attending the opening show of an abstract artist in a gallery in New York. She is standing sipping a glass of Chardonnay in front of a large abstract painting full of bright reds, oranges, and yellows that appear splashed all over the canvas.

While she is standing there staring curiously at this canvas, the new artist strolls up and haughtily asks, "How do you like my painting?"

The little old lady turns and stares at him, then stares back at the painting, and then turns back to him and asks, "What is it?"

In a superior tone of voice, the artist says, "Well, it's supposed to be a sunset."

The little old lady looks at him directly and says, "Then, why ain't it?"

The point of this story is simple. Any piece of artwork, commercial design, or packaging should be simple, clear, and straightforward. It should be absolutely obvious to the casual observer glancing at your product packaging what is in the package. Closer inspection of the package should give at least one specific reason to buy, a benefit or an advantage that the purchaser will enjoy if he or she buys this product or service. It should be so clear that a 10-year-old child should be able to look at the package and then turn to another 10-year-old and tell him or her why anyone should buy this product or service.

Awards for Failure

Each year, the advertising industry holds its version of the Academy Awards ceremony, the Clio Awards. These awards are given to advertising agencies and commercial artists for what the advertising industry considers to be the very best advertisements that appeared in the previous year.

Every year, almost without exception, when the six art awards are given for the best packaging or artistic design for a product, it turns out that fully five of those products have already *failed* completely in the marketplace. In some cases, the company that bought this wonderful advertising and packaging actually went bankrupt as the result of the "commercial art concept" that it had purchased to promote the product.

Differences Make a Difference

When Lexus and Infiniti entered the U.S. market in the same year, they were both beautifully designed, mid-level luxury Japanese cars. They were both loaded with features and benefits that made them enormously attractive and appealing. They both had the same goal, to crack the U.S. market for cars at this price level and sell a large number of their product.

J.D. Powers, the people who conduct customer satisfaction surveys in the auto industry, soon rated both the Lexus and the Infiniti as two of the best cars sold in America, according to customers.

Nonetheless, the Lexus people sold their cars in one way and the Infiniti people chose another way. First of all, Lexus set up separate dealerships for their cars. Even though Lexus is owned by Toyota, Toyota dealerships were not allowed to sell the new models. They then focused on straightforward, hard-hitting, benefit-oriented advertising and promotion. They attracted people to the dealerships to test-drive the cars. They sold them by the thousands and then by the tens of thousands.

Infiniti, produced by Nissan, took a different route. Nissan decided to create a Zen-like dealership where customers would hear the gentle trickling of water and see bonsai trees neatly groomed around the showroom. The salespeople were calm and relaxed, as though they had just come out of a meditation session. The customers were encouraged to browse slowly and gently around the dealership and, if they had any desire for a car, they could talk with one of the nice gentleman or ladies lounging on the edges of the dealership.

Needless to say, this concept failed miserably. American buyers are accustomed to coming in, asking a salesperson questions, taking the car for a test-drive, negotiating the final price and driving away, sometimes all within one hour.

With the Infiniti dealerships, customers were encouraged to think things through on their own, to enjoy the quiet, meditative space of the dealership, and to seek out a salesperson if it occurred to them to buy a car.

Listen to Your Inner Voice

The bottom line of this discussion about the outside packaging and appearance of every element of your company is that you must trust your *intuition*. You must trust your personal judgment. You must look at every product or service packaging idea from the point of view of your own experience and wisdom. You must ask, "Based on this look or appearance, would I buy it personally?"

Compare yourself with your very best competitors. Visit their stores and places of business. Look at their offices and their furniture. Look at their people and their promotions. Look at their advertisements of all kinds.

When you enter into a competitive market, your goal must be to make your packaging equal to or better than your best competitors in the market. Your goal must be to be in the top 10 percent of companies and industries in your field.

Your Place of Business

Bill and Susan enrolled in my one-year Focal Point Advanced Coaching and Mentoring Program, coming to San Diego to work with me intensively for one day every three months. Step by step, we showed them how to improve their marketing, focus on higher-income activities, delegate and outsource low-value tasks, and reorganize both their lives and work so they could earn more money and take more time off simultaneously.

During our second full-day meeting, they took me aside and asked my advice on a problem that was perplexing them. They said, "Our marketing and advertising systems are quite effective in attracting new prospective clients to our offices. But once they visit our offices, only one out of ten of them decides to purchase our services. We simply can't figure out why our closing ratio is so low."

I said to them, "Let me guess. You started off your business in your home. When you moved to business offices, you gathered up some old furniture for your reception area and fixed up your offices on the cheap?"

Susan immediately turned to Bill and said angrily, "I told you so."

It turned out that when they were operating out of their house, they went out to see their clients almost all of the time. When they moved to their offices, they encouraged their clients to visit them. But their offices were poorly furnished and poorly decorated and looked both cheap and disorganized.

They decided at that minute to invest some money to make their premises look attractive and professional.

When they returned three months later, they had an incredible story to tell. They had invested about $4,000 in furnishing their reception area so that it looked beautiful. They put in attractive furniture, carpets, repainted the walls, hung pictures, and piped in gentle classical music.

And, to their surprise and delight, their closing ratio with new prospective clients had jumped from one in ten to eight in ten. Their income had increased 400 percent. Almost everyone who visited them became a client. They were still amazed at the incredible difference that a change in the appearance of their offices had made.

On the way to wealth, you must continually stand back from your products, services, and place of business and view them as if you were a third party—a customer, a competitor, or a consultant that you had hired to help you with your business.

Looking through these eyes, does your business give an immediate impression of a first-class, competent, high-quality organization? Do people walk into your place of business, take one look around, and decide that this is where they want to spend their money? Do your customers and clients compliment you regularly on how nice your offices or place of business looks?

Be your own toughest critic. Is it time to move uptown?

Remember: your customers have made hundreds of buying mistakes. They are absolutely determined not to make another buying mistake. Because of the jumbled emotions that people have about parting with their money, they are looking for reasons to *exclude* you, not *include* you.

Everything Counts

Credibility is everything—and everything counts. You must invest whatever time, money, and effort is necessary to make your premises look as good as or better than those of any of your competitors.

Can you imagine increasing your closing ratio from one in ten to eight in ten? Can you calculate what a difference that would make in your sales, revenues, and profits? Can you imagine achieving this kind of improvement in profits simply by changing some of the visual aspects of your place of business?

Think like a Big Business

There is a rule that a small business should think like a big business. The big, successful businesses have all been through this thinking process and arrived at the same point of decision. They have carefully examined every single factor that influences their customers in any way, especially the visual factors.

As a result, they are absolutely determined to make sure that every moment of truth with a customer or prospective customer is a positive one. They take no prisoners. They are adamant about the packaging of their products and their people, the look of every single piece of stationery or promotional material they distribute, and the appearance of their premises. They pay careful attention to each detail. They know that everything counts.

Think Back from the Future

Imagine that you have started and built a very successful business. You have tremendous sales and high levels of customer satisfaction. Revenues and profits are great, the money just rolls in, and you are already a self-made millionaire or a multimillionaire.

From this mental vantage point, think about how your business would look and operate if it were already a tremendous success in a competitive market. As I mentioned before, this is called "back from the future thinking."

First, you project forward in your mind to an *ideal future state*, one where you are completely successful in every area of your business.

Then, from this ideal future picture, you look back to where you are today. You imagine the changes you would make and the steps you would take to create a beautiful business.

What would you do first? What would you do second? What would you start doing that you are not doing today? What would you stop doing? This "back from the future thinking" and the practice of visualizing your ideal picture of your business will give you insights and ideas that you can apply immediately to making every part of your business appealing and attractive to your prospects and customers.

The finest product or service in the world, if it is presented and packaged poorly, will not sell. On the other hand, an average product or service, if presented beautifully, will sell in large quantities. Packaging is vitally important. And everything counts!

Action Exercises

1. Begin with yourself. Do you dress, groom, and look like a successful, millionaire entrepreneur business owner? If not, what changes are you going to make immediately?

2. Look at your staff. Do they look so good that you are proud to introduce them to your customers and bankers as representatives of your business?

3. Look at your personal office. Ask, "What kind of a person sits at that desk, drives that car, or works in that kind of environment?"

4. Visit the businesses of your best competitors. Does your place of business look as good as or better than they do?

5. Look at your stationery, business cards, and brochure. Do they shout out the message, "Quality! Reliability! Value! Trustworthiness!" to everyone who sees them?

6. Look at your product packaging. Does it suggest quality and value to your customers?

7. Resolve today to make every visual element of your business as attractive as it would be if your business were already in the *Fortune* 500.

CHAPTER SIX

Get Your Numbers Right

"The successful person makes a habit of doing what the failing person doesn't like to do."

—*Thomas Edison*

Your ability to do accurate costing for your products and services, and then to set proper prices for what you sell, can make all the difference between profits and losses, success and failure.

The name of the game is "profit." Everything you do in your business, every number that you calculate and consider, every point of focus and concentration must be aimed at generating profits of some kind.

Profits can be defined as "the excess of revenues over costs." You earn a profit when you sell a product or service at a price that is greater than the total cost of bringing that product or service to market. Always remember the Japanese proverb,

"Making money is like digging in the sand with a pin; losing money is like pouring water on the sand."

Become a Numbers Person

Most entrepreneurs are motivated by ideas, concepts, hopes, desires, and optimism. They like to interact with people, to market and sell. They enjoy negotiating, communicating, and persuading. They are action-oriented and like to be in continuous motion. They start early, work hard, and stay late. Often entrepreneurs will work for months and years, seven days a week, 10, 12, and 14 hours per day to turn their dreams of entrepreneurial success into reality.

But most entrepreneurs are not "numbers" people. They have little patience for the details of financial statements and accounting. They are eager to get on with the business of meeting with people and selling the product. In fact, for most entrepreneurs, dealing with numbers is irritating and frustrating.

> **M**ost entrepreneurs are not "numbers" people. They have little patience for the details of financial statements and accounting.

Nonetheless, for you to move solidly along the way to wealth, to become a successful entrepreneur, and eventually, a self-made millionaire, you must master the numbers in your business. You can hire bookkeepers, accountants and financial advisors to help you, but you can never abdicate the responsibility of fully understanding every penny and every dollar that comes in and out of your business.

Get the Facts

Harold Geneen of ITT once said, *"Get the facts. Get the real facts. Not the hoped-for facts, the assumed facts, or the possible facts. Get the real facts. Facts don't lie."*

It is absolutely essential for your success that you know the financial facts of every aspect of your business, especially your costs to produce and offer your product or service and the prices you charge for what you sell. It is amazing how many businesses, large and small, are operating on the basis of false assumptions and incorrect numbers. Sometimes they joke and say, "We lose money on everything we sell, but we make it up on the volume." But this is not a joke.

Determining Your Costs

Often the person who makes the fewest mistakes in business is the one who succeeds the most. You don't have to be an entrepreneurial genius to be successful. You just have to master your numbers and know what you are doing.

You have heard the old saying, "You can't get there from here." When you do an accurate cost analysis for a new product or service, you will often find that, based on what you can charge for that product or service in the current market, you can't make a profit on it. It makes no sense to go through all the time and trouble of bringing this product to market because the return is too low. The potential for loss is too high. The possible profits are not as great as you could earn by offering something else.

One of the keys to entrepreneurial success is to offer a high-margin product or service of some kind. It is to produce, acquire, sell, or distribute a product or service from which you earn high profits on the sale of each one. In this way, you have a substantial cushion built in to protect you from losses. With high profit margins, you might fail to meet your optimistic sales projections and go over budget in unexpected areas, but you will still end up with more profit than losses at the end of the day.

Be Brutally Honest with Yourself

In determining your costs, you must be brutally honest with yourself. You must include every single cost that will be incurred in the process of satisfying your customer. You must include the costs of the product; the costs of marketing, advertising, and selling the product; the costs of delivering and servicing the product; and the after-sales costs of repairs, maintenance, and returns for any reason. Once you have totaled up all of these costs, you should then add a "fudge factor" of 10 percent or 20 percent to give yourself a buffer against unexpected costs that will pop up in spite of your best efforts to avoid them.

There are several costs that you must consider.

1. **Direct costs.** These are the *costs of goods sold*. If you make a product or buy it from a manufacturer or distributor for $5, including all costs of shipping, transportation, insurance, and delivery, and you sell the product for $10, your cost of goods sold is $5. This is fairly easy to calculate.

2. **Indirect costs.** These are the costs that are *attributable* to all of the products or services that you sell, not any specific ones. Indirect costs can be costs of salaries, rent, telephones, utilities, marketing, advertising, shipping, delivery, and many others.

Specialist companies make a good living by going into businesses and analyzing the true direct and indirect costs of producing and selling each product or service. Many business owners are astonished to find that a product that they thought was profitable is actually costing them money each time they sell an item because of "unattributed costs."

Include Every Expense

Upon inspection, it may turn out that the cost of executive time, staff salaries, advertising, sales costs and commissions, shipping and delivery, insurance, and returns because of product defects or dissatisfied customers actually total up to a loss on every sale. This is why it is so important that you continually calculate and recalculate every dollar that you must spend per product or service that you sell.

You need to consider the costs of returns, both shipping and delivery. You need to calculate "shrinkage," the cost of your products or services that "disappear" in the course of business activities. You need to calculate breakage and defects. You need to calculate losses that come from writing off accounts from people who cannot or will not pay you for what you have sold them. In totaling your indirect costs, you need to determine how much you must allocate for follow-up services, maintenance, and repairs for the product or service you sell.

In addition, you must calculate the outside services that you require to operate your business, especially legal and accounting. And you must calculate not only the labor costs and salaries of each staff member who must spend any amount of time producing, selling, or delivering any product or service, but you must also include *your own labor* at your hourly rate.

The average entrepreneur works about 2,000 hours per year. If your income target is $50,000 per year, divide it by 2,000 to get your desired hourly rate of $25. If your income goal is $100,000 per year, your hourly rate is $50. In determining your indirect costs, you must include the number of hours of your individual time that go into achieving the ultimate sale. Otherwise, your true costs will be distorted and inaccurate.

3. Fixed costs. These are the costs that you incur each month whether or not you sell a single item or generate a single dollar of revenue. Your fixed costs include salaries for your permanent staff, rent, utilities, many operational costs, and the costs for outside services, plus your own personal income from the business.

You should calculate your fixed costs regularly to determine how much it costs you to stay in business if you have no revenues at all. One of your business goals should be to continually find ways to reduce your fixed costs.

4. Variable costs. These are the costs that increase or decrease depending on your level of business activity. These costs are incurred only when a sale takes place. They can include costs of goods sold, sales commissions, delivery costs, and other costs that can be attributed, directly or indirectly, to the cost of each product or service you sell.

5. Semi-variable costs. These are costs that are partially fixed and partially variable. They can include part-time labor when you are busier than normal, additional utility, telephone, and mailing costs, and additional costs for outside services.

6. Sunk costs. These are expenses that you have incurred that are *gone forever*. They can never be recovered. They are like an unattached anchor thrown overboard that sinks to the bottom of the ocean and is irretrievable.

Here's an important point. Many entrepreneurs make the mistake of attempting to retrieve their sunk costs. For example, they place an advertisement that generates no response. They then decide to place even more advertisements of the same kind, in the same medium, in order to "capitalize" on the amount they have already lost with an ineffective advertising campaign. They "throw good money after bad." We often refer to this as "pouring money down a rat hole."

> Many entrepreneurs make the mistake of attempting to retrieve their sunk costs.

Ambrose Bierce once wrote, "Fanaticism consists of redoubling your efforts when you have forgotten your aim."

Building a business is often a sloppy affair. No matter how smart you are, you will buy products that you cannot resell, that no one wants at any price. You will buy furniture that will turn out to be of no value to you. You will run advertisements and engage in other costs that, in retrospect, were a complete waste of money. In building a business, these mistakes are inevitable.

But it is essential that you recognize them for what they are—sunk costs. The money is gone forever. You cannot recoup it. You must not spend a single dollar attempting to compensate for a financial mistake in the past. Focus on the future and on sales and profits. Let the sunk costs go.

Once you have accurately calculated all of these expenses, direct and indirect, fixed and variable, plus semi-variable, you will have a precise cost for bringing each product or service to the market satisfactorily. With this number, you can then begin thinking about your pricing structure.

Pricing Your Products

Sometimes I ask a group of business owners, "Who sets your prices? Who determines your profit margins? Who determines what you offer, to whom you offer it, and how much you sell? Who determines the entire course of your business in a competitive market?"

Almost invariably, the first response I get is "I do!"

Then, I gently point out that this is not true. I tell them, "In reality, your competition determines how much you charge, how much you sell, who you sell it to, your profit margins, how fast you grow, and almost everything else about your business."

Business Is Like Warfare

Business is like warfare in a certain way. In warfare, most strategy is determined by the enemy. It is determined by what you need to do to defeat your enemy and what your enemy is likely to do to counter your actions in order to defeat you.

As an entrepreneur, you must be looking in two directions simultaneously. You must be intensely focused on your customers, on who they are, where they are, what they want and need, what they will pay for, how they buy, and every other factor about them. At the same time, you must be intensely focused on your competitors. Remember: your competitors get up every single morning and think all day long about how to *put you out of business.* They think about how to undercut your prices and steal your customers. Just as you are focused on sales and profits, so are they. From the day you begin thinking about being an entrepreneur, your competitors will have a major influence on every decision you make and how successful those decisions turn out to be.

Your Goal in Business

Your goal in business is to achieve a "meaningful and sustainable competitive advantage." This means that you build into your product or service specific benefits and advantages to the customer that no one else offers. You create or discover your "unique selling proposition." You then seek out those specific customers in the marketplace who want, need, and are willing to pay the very most for what it is that you do or offer better than anyone else. This is the key to business success.

> Your goal in business is to achieve a "meaningful and sustainable competitive advantage."

Nonetheless, you need to think carefully about your *prices*. Prices are subjective. There are no hard and fast rules for setting prices on a product or service. There are only "guesstimates" of what customers will pay and of what the market will bear. Your job is to determine a price that is the very highest price possible that you can charge without losing your customers to your competitors.

The Market Clearing Price

In economics, there is a concept called the "market-clearing price." This is the price at which all buyers can purchase all the products or services of a particular kind that they want and at which all sellers can sell all the products or services that they offer. At the end of the day, everyone is satisfied: all buyers have purchased everything they want and all sellers have sold everything they have offered. This is the ideal price, the market-clearing price, in any market.

Whenever you see a discount sale at any business, and especially in retail operations, you see an example where the people who priced the products guessed *wrong*. They set a price that was too high to enable them to sell all they had to offer to buyers at that price. As a result, they are forced to guess again. They must lower the price and attempt once more to clear their stock and recoup their investment.

Sometimes you see a store that will offer more than one series of discounts. They will have a sale, and then another sale at even lower prices. In each case, the storeowners are guessing again and again. They are struggling to find the price at which they can clear their stock, the price at which sellers will buy all they have to offer.

Never Be Overstocked

One of the reasons that Wal-Mart is the most successful retail operation in the world is because of their policy of "Always low prices." Because of their highly sophisticated, satellite-controlled inventory and distribution systems, they are never overstocked in any store.

Every purchase at a Wal-Mart store is immediately communicated by satellite to massive company computers in Bentonville, Arkansas. This information concerning product, size, color, and characteristic is immediately conveyed, again by satellite, to the manufacturers and shippers of the products nationally or internationally. Each factory has up-to-date feedback on exactly which products to produce and exactly which stores to ship them to and in exactly what quantity, color, kind, type or shape. Wal-Mart is successful largely because it has the most sophisticated distribution system of any retail operation in the world.

When you shop at Wal-Mart, you know that it is unlikely that Wal-Mart will be discounting that product in a clearance sale a couple of weeks from now. You also know that, because of Wal-Mart's ability to purchase in massive quantities, you are probably getting the best price possible for that particular item. As a result, people shop at Wal-Mart with complete confidence, to the tune of almost $300 billion per year.

Pricing Models

There are various ways that you can set your prices for your products or services. But you must always remember that these are "guesstimates" based on your knowledge of what your competition is charging and what your customers are likely to pay, combined with your intuition, your gut feeling, about what the market will bear.

The "entrepreneurial instinct" that makes you successful is your ability to perceive a gap between what customers will pay for your product or service and the total cost of bringing that product or service to the market. It is this "profit opportunity" that entrepreneurs can see, and that most other people cannot see, that is the spark that triggers entrepreneurial activity. The better you become at identifying this gap between sales price and cost, the more successful you become as an entrepreneur.

Cost Plus Markup

In this model of pricing, you take your total cost for a product or service and mark it up by a specific amount, usually a percentage.

For example, in restaurants it is standard to mark up a bottle of wine 100 percent. If the bottle costs $25 from the wholesaler, the restaurant puts it on the menu at $50.

Depending upon competitive pressures and sales volume, companies will mark up their products with different percentages. For jewelry, for example, because jewelry stores have to carry such large inventories, the markups can be several hundred percent. For groceries, because products turn over so fast, the markups are about 20 percent of wholesale costs. This is a convenient way to set your prices, especially at the beginning. But always keep your competitors' prices in mind.

Cost Plus

When I built my first shopping center, the owner of the construction company explained to me their pricing practice. They said, "We take the total cost of construction and then add 10 percent for administration and 10 percent for profit."

This is cost-plus pricing. Many companies that offer services will total the entire cost, direct and indirect, of providing the service and then mark it up by a fixed percentage. Many contracts, large and small, are done on a cost-plus basis. This might be appropriate for your business, as well.

Multiple of Total Costs

You calculate your total costs of production, or costs of goods sold, and then multiply that by a specific number. If you manufacture a high-margin product or service, you could mark it up by five or even ten times the manufacturing cost. This is quite common.

> If you manufacture a high-margin product or service, you could mark it up by five or even ten times the manufacturing cost.

For example, in book publishing, the retail price of the book is usually equal to seven times the cost of printing the book. If the book costs $3 to print, the retail price in the bookstore will be $21. This is the rule of thumb used in the publishing industry.

Many entrepreneurs do not realize that, because of all of the indirect and unexpected costs in their businesses, they can go broke marking up a product by 100 percent. They can buy a product for $10 and sell it for $20. But once they have deducted all of the various costs that go into getting that product to the customer, they find that they are losing money on every sale. Don't let this happen to you.

Market Pricing

This is perhaps the most common way of setting a price on a commonly used consumer product. Unless your product or service offers a valuable benefit not offered by your competitors, you will have to keep your prices within 10 percent of what your competitors are charging for the same product or service in the same market area.

When I was working in the banking and trust industry, they offered a certain percentage return on fixed deposits. Customers are hypersensitive to even quarter-point increases or decreases in these amounts. All a bank or trust company had to do to increase its deposits immediately was to raise the interest rate that it was paying by one quarter of a point. In a short time, millions of dollars of new deposits would flow to that institution.

In self-storage, for example, the amounts that can be charged for a specific size of storage unit in a particular area are quite uniform throughout that area. People who store their possessions will move from one place to another for a difference in rent of as little as $5 a month. Again, competition sets the prices that you can charge.

Monopoly Prices

These are prices that you can charge because no one else offers the same product or service as you in that market area. As a result, you can charge premium prices, prices that are highly profitable to you, and customers who want your product or service have no choice but to pay you what you demand.

The ability to charge monopoly or above-market prices comes about only because your product or service is unique and irreplaceable. For example, you can often charge monopoly prices simply because of your geographical location, which no one else has.

Convenience stores charge substantially more for their products than large grocery stores. They can do this because they have a monopoly on their location. They are the only store close to the customer and therefore are a quick and convenient place at which to shop. They commonly mark up what they sell by 30 percent to 50 percent and customers willingly pay it.

One of the ways that you can charge monopoly prices is by designing or structuring your products or services in such a way that they are far more attractive and desirable than those of your competitors. You, in fact, become the "only" choice for a potential customer. The customer cannot think of going anywhere else except to your place of business.

In professional speaking, there are thousands of speakers who give talks and seminars on every conceivable subject. The average speaker or trainer may earn a few hundred dollars per day for all the work of travel, preparation, and delivery.

But in this industry, there are "marquee" speakers such as Colin Powell, Norman Schwarzkopf, Bill Clinton, and sports stars who commonly demand and get fees of $50,000, $100,000, and even $150,000 for a keynote talk of less than one hour.

Why is this? It is because there is only one of each of them. Each is a monopoly. If a person wants that speaker, there are no alternatives. If a company or organization wants to book Bill Clinton or George H.W. Bush to speak, it has no choice but to pay the monopoly price.

One of the questions that you must continually ask is "How can I structure my business or my offerings in such a way that I am the pre-eminent choice for customers in my market?"

What can you do to make your products or services so attractive that your prospective customers see you as the very best choice of all, the *only* choice, all things considered? By asking and answering this question continually, you may come up with a special way of doing business that gives you a competitive advantage. This then enables you to charge premium prices and earn premium profits.

Variable Prices

Many companies charge different prices, at different times, for different reasons, for the same product or service. Their prices vary depending upon circumstances.

For example, if you sell a single product or service to a single customer, your costs can be quite high in servicing that customer. In this case, you would charge "full retail."

On the other hand, if your customer were to buy a *large volume* of your products or services, your cost of servicing that customer would decline dramatically. In this case, you could offer substantial discounts for volume purchases, as many companies do.

You could offer variable prices if people purchased from you more frequently. Frequent flier programs are built around offering bonuses, upgrades, and special services to encourage travelers to use a particular airline more often.

Many companies charge variable prices based on the time of day, week, or even season or year that people buy. For example, if you buy ski equipment in the fall prior to the ski season, prices will be at their peaks. If, on the other hand, you buy ski equipment in the spring and summer, after the ski season, you can buy at substantially reduced prices.

If you go to a vacation resort during the holiday season, the prices will be at their maximum levels. If you visit the same vacation resort during the off-season, the prices are substantially lower.

Many restaurants offer special bonuses, discounts, and two-for-one offers for people who dine on Monday, Tuesday, or Wednesday. Some restaurants offer half-priced bottles of wine on slow nights to attract more customers and to help offset their fixed costs.

Often, companies will have spare capacity. They will have fixed costs of equipment, staff, rent, utilities, and other costs that must be paid. To defray these costs, they will often offer their products or services at deeply discounted prices, just above their total costs, in order to keep the staff working and the factories operating.

In car dealerships, the salespeople are assigned monthly quotas. At the beginning of the month, the quota period has just begun. They will therefore bargain very hard. The salespeople will make every effort to charge you the highest possible price if you go out to buy a car in the first three weeks of the month. Toward the end of the month, the pressure to make quota increases and the salespeople will make whatever concessions are necessary to make a sale. If you are going to buy a car, always go during the last few days of the month. You get the best prices and conditions possible.

Another type of variable price sale is the "add-on" or "upsell." In this case, you can offer your product or service at a special price, as long as the customer at the same time buys something else, on which you also make a profit. For example, Xerox used to sell its copiers at low prices just as long as the customers bought all their high-priced paper from the company, which made most of its profit from the paper, not the copiers.

> With upsell, you can offer your product or service at a special price, as long as the customer at the same time buys something else, on which you also make a profit.

Consider the hospitality industry as another example. If you want to reserve a hotel room, always phone the hotel *directly*. Do not use the 800 number. People who answer the 800 number, the national reservation service, have no flexibility to negotiate rates.

When you phone the hotel directly, ask for the "very best rate" for a room on the dates that you desire. The first price that the employee will give you will be the "full rack rate," the highest possible rate for that room.

You then ask, "Do you have a lower rate?"

If the hotel is not full for the dates when you want a room, the employees are instructed not to let you off the line. They are taught and trained to get you to reserve a room, at any price. They know that an empty hotel room is of no value to them at all.

When you ask for a lower rate, they will suggest a corporate rate or a rate for a room without much of a view. You then ask again if they have a lower rate than *that*. They will then move down to an even lower rate. With many hotels that are not fully booked, you can continue this process down through as many as seven discounts. This is another form of variable pricing, where they will make every effort not to lose the potential customer.

The Walkaway Price

This is the price *below which* you will not sell your product or service. You should be clear about this number before you begin negotiating. This becomes the basis for your variable pricing. Below this amount, you incur losses that make it of no value for you to offer the product or service at all.

Introductory or Loss Leader Prices

With this type of pricing, you consider the *lifetime value* of a customer. If you know from experience that a customer who buys from you will buy from you several times over the coming months or years, you can often charge a "loss leader price" to acquire the customer. This discount is simply a cost of doing business, a cost of "buying" a customer.

In many cases, it is quite common, especially for retail or service businesses, to lose money on the first sale. Because of the high costs of marketing, advertising, and selling commissions or expenses, plus the cost of goods sold, a business can actually end up with a net loss on a sale once all your costs have been deducted. There's often no choice but to do this.

However, when you calculate the lifetime value of the customer and you are confident that this customer, if satisfied, will buy from you over and over again, you can justify taking a loss on the first sale.

It is quite common for professional services firms to offer their services at a 50 percent discount for the first year, if the client will sign a five-year contract. They will

It is quite common for professional services firms to offer their services at a 50 percent discount for the first year, if the client will sign a five-year contract.

lose money the first time they do business with the client, but they will make it up later. In the meantime, they will keep their people, facilities, and resources busy during the initial period.

Market Demand Pricing

This is charging whatever you feel that the market will pay. If you have a competitive advantage of some kind, you can charge a premium because customers will willingly pay more to get the special features or benefits that you offer. After the Hurricane Katrina disaster, for example, prices for hotels, food, transportation, and many other products of limited supply increased all over the surrounding area because of the sudden surge in demand.

When should you raise your prices? The best time is when the market demand for your products or services is almost greater than your capacity to deliver them.

If you are a service company and you are fully booked, all day long, you can probably raise your prices without decreasing the demand. If people are buying your products with both hands and you cannot keep enough of them in stock, this is a good sign that your products are *underpriced* based on what customers are willing to pay. In this case, you can gradually raise your prices, selectively or across the board. You continue raising your prices for your products or services until the demand slows down and balances out with the quantity of products and services that you are prepared to supply.

Breakeven Price

This is the price at which you earn neither a profit nor a loss. You sell the product for exactly what it cost you to produce it. You only sell at the breakeven price when you cannot charge any more, and you do not have to charge any less.

Clearance Sale Price

This is the price at which you admit that the market demand for the product or service you have produced is considerably less than you had anticipated. You have too many of your products in stock. They are taking up too much room and selling too slowly.

At the clearance sale price, you bite the bullet and realize that "Half a loaf is better than none." You clear out your stock so that you can turn that "dead stock" into cash that you can then use to offer other products and services that are in greater demand and on which you can earn a greater profit.

Pricing Flexibility

This is an *attitude* more than anything else. Always remember that prices are subjective. They are guesses at what the market will bear. They are based on a variety of pieces of information that are continually changing.

You want to sell as many of your products and services as possible, at the highest possible price, to yield the highest possible profits. But from the beginning to the end of your entrepreneurial career, you must always be flexible with your prices and be prepared and willing to raise or lower them depending on market conditions.

Sometimes, you can increase your prices by a large or small amount and dramatically change the profitability of your business. In other cases, you can lower the price of your products or services and so increase your sales volume at a lower profit point such that your overall profits increase substantially.

For example, if you are selling 1,000 units per month at $10 and making a profit of $3 each, you would be earning $3,000 per month in profit. But if you lowered your price to $9, you might sell 2,000 units per month and earn $4,000 (2,000 x $2 profit per item). In each case, it is a judgment call that you must continually test and measure.

The key is to be *flexible*. Nothing is written in stone. Be open to new information. Be continually watching your competition. Listen closely to your customers. Keep your hand on the pulse of the sales and profitability of your business.

Breakeven Pricing

This is one of the most important numbers that you must calculate for every product and service that you offer. Fortunately, it is not particularly difficult, if you have done the proper costing and pricing exercises described above.

In breakeven pricing, you first determine the total cost of bringing your product or service to market. If you have a variety of products or services, you calculate the total costs of each one, using the formulas described earlier.

Once you know how much your product or service costs, you then determine exactly how much you can sell it for in a competitive market. You take into consideration all of the volume purchase discounts, losses, breakage, shrinkage, defects, returns, and all other deductions from your sales prices and work out the exact *average* price that you receive for the sale of each item.

To determine your breakeven point, you then deduct your total average costs per item from the total average selling price per item. This gives you your *profit contribution*.

Calculate Your Profit Margin

Your profit contribution is also your *profit margin*, often expressed as a percentage. This gives you the exact amount of *gross profit* or *return on sales* that you earn from each sale.

You then total your fixed costs of operation. Remember: these are the amounts that you have to pay each month, whether you make a sale or not. You divide your average profit contribution per item into your monthly fixed costs to determine your breakeven point.

For example, if your average gross profit per item sold is $10 and your fixed costs of operation are $10,000 per month, you divide $10 into $10,000 to get a breakeven point of 1,000 units.

This means that you have to sell 1,000 units of your product each month to break even. Below that point, you are losing money each month. Above that point, you are earning a gross profit of $10 per item sold.

Reduce Your Fixed Costs

Your goal throughout your business career is to reduce your fixed costs and increase your variable costs. You reduce the costs that you have to pay each month, whether you make a sale or not, and increase your variable costs, the amounts that you have to pay *only* when you make sales.

> Your goal throughout your business career is to reduce your fixed costs and increase your variable costs.

By doing this, you lower your breakeven point as far as you can. The *lower* your breakeven point, the fewer number of units you have to sell each month before you make a profit.

Evaluate Every Expenditure

Once you have determined your breakeven point, you evaluate every expenditure against this number. If you are going to advertise, you determine how many of your units you will have to sell in order to break even on a particular form of advertising at a particular cost. If you are going to buy any type of equipment to improve the operations of your business, you calculate how many more of your products you will have to sell in order to break even on that investment. You apply your breakeven number to every amount that you anticipate spending, for any reason, to grow your business. This is one of the best "reality checks" you will ever use as an entrepreneur.

Financial Ratios

To be a successful entrepreneur, you must have a firm grasp of the numbers in your business. Over the years, several financial ratios have been developed as tools to help business owners understand the numbers in their businesses with greater clarity.

1. Gross margin. This is the amount of profit that you earn after deducting the cost of goods sold and all other direct costs involved in producing and delivering your product or service to your customer.

2. Net margin. This is the amount of net profit that you earn per sale or per month after deducting all of the direct, indirect, and attributable costs involved in operating your business.

For example, grocery stores mark up the products they sell by an average of 20 percent. But the average net profit that grocery stores earn on sales is closer to 3 percent. The difference is eaten up by all of the costs involved in running a grocery store.

The average large company in America earns less than 10 percent net profit, usually closer to 5 percent, after all costs of operation have been deducted. This is often called *EBITDA* (earnings before interest, taxes, depreciation, and amortization) or sometimes *EBTIDA* (earnings before taxes, interest, depreciation, and amortization).

Remember: small increases in prices and small reductions in costs can lead to huge differences in profitability. Every dollar that you save in cost reduction goes straight to the bottom line as net profit. Every dollar that you earn in increased prices, holding costs constant, goes straight to the bottom line, as well.

3. Return on investment (ROI). This is the total profit, expressed as a percentage, that you earn based on the total amount invested in your business. This total amount includes the money that you have paid out of your own pocket, plus all of the other money that has been invested or borrowed in any way.

4. Return on equity (ROE). This is the percentage return that you earn on the money that you have personally invested in the business. This is usually a more accurate way of determining the profitability of your enterprise.

For example, if you have invested $100,000 of your own money in the business and you are earning a net profit of $10,000 per year, your return on equity is 10 percent. Whenever you calculate potential returns on investment or returns on equity, you must always compare the return from this business activity with the return from any other business activity in which you can invest the same amount of time, money. and energy.

5. Return on sales (ROS). This is another way of calculating your gross margin. It is the percentage of gross profit that you make from each sale. If you buy an item for $1 and you sell it for $2, your *return on sales* would be 50 percent.

6. Return on energy (ROE). This is perhaps the most important calculation of all. This is the return you receive on the amount of physical, mental, and emotional energy you invest in your business. Sometimes this is referred to as your *return on life*. You must be continually aware of how much of your life you are investing in your business. Financial investments can be recouped or replaced, but the amount of your life that you spend on any business activity is gone forever.

Analyze and Compare

The reason that you continually calculate your gross margins, net margins, and return on sales is to *compare* the various products and services that you offer. The 80/20 rule says that 20 percent of your products and services will yield 80 percent of your profits. You must be absolutely clear which products and services are the most profitable for you to offer. These financial ratios help you develop that clarity.

Watch Your Numbers

In this chapter, we have discussed the most important numbers for you to know and understand in building a successful business on your way to wealth.

Before you make any business decision or investment, you should take the time to achieve complete *accuracy* with regard to the amount you can charge, the

> Before you make any business decision or investment, you should take the time to achieve complete *accuracy* with regard to the amount you can charge.

prices that people will pay for your products or services, and the exact cost of bringing those products or services to market.

You must be clear about your *breakeven point* and continually update and evaluate this breakeven point as market conditions, prices, and costs change.

You should continually evaluate your business in terms of your return on sales, your return on equity, your return on investment, your gross and net margins, and the actual amount that you take home at the end of the day, your return on energy.

You must always include your personal labor as a key cost of doing business. Without your investment of mental, emotional, and physical energy, there would be no business.

Many business owners earn less operating their own businesses than they would if they worked for someone else. Because they do not include the cost of their labor as a real cost of doing business, they understate their costs and expenses and often underprice their products and services. Don't let this happen to you.

Get a Good Accountant

Get a good accountant to calculate these numbers for you. Review them regularly. Be continually looking for ways to reduce costs and increase prices. Be continually seeking ways to increase gross and net margins on everything you sell.

The good news is that the more time and attention that you devote to studying and understanding your financial statements and ratios, the better you will get in this area. The better you get, the better decisions you will make. The better decisions you make, the more profitable your business will become and the faster you will move along the way to wealth.

Action Exercises

1. Calculate for your best-selling product or service exactly how much you receive per sale and how much it costs to service your customer.

2. Examine each of your better-selling products or services and determine if you should raise or lower your prices.

3. Calculate your fixed costs for your business, including your own time, so you know what it costs you to keep your doors open.

4. Calculate the breakeven point for your business and seek ways to lower it each month.

5. Decide what constitutes a "sunk cost" and resolve today not to spend another dollar or minute trying to recoup it.

6. Calculate your own personal hourly rate and compare every activity you engage in against that amount.

7. Decide today to take action in at least one area to increase your prices, make your products more attractive, or reduce your fixed costs.

CHAPTER SEVEN

Increasing Your Profits

Go out and buy yourself a five-cent pencil and a ten-cent notebook and begin to write down some million-dollar ideas for yourself.

—Bob Grinde

Your ability to generate profits in your business is the critical determinant of your success. It must be the focal point of all your efforts. It must be the guiding principle for all your decisions. The purpose of all your business activities is to create and keep customers at a profit.

Begin by imagining that it is possible for you to *double your profits* in your business and then double them again. Whatever your profits were in the last month or year (assuming that your business was profitable), imagine earning twice as much. In the coming pages, you will learn strategies, techniques, and methods that you can use to achieve this goal, over and over.

Every Business Starts Small

Every large business started as a small business, often with a single person who had a single product or service idea. That individual then did a series of things that enabled his or her business to survive, first of all, and then to thrive.

Whether it was Michael Dell assembling computers for his classmates in his dorm room at the University of Texas in Austin, or William Hewlett and David Packard building a small oscilloscope in a garage in Palo Alto, California, every big business was once a small business.

The law of cause and effect says that there is a reason for everything. Every effect has a cause or a series of causes of some kind. This law says that if you can be clear about the effect that you want (in this case, profits), you can then look around and find another company or companies that once wanted to be profitable and achieved it. If you then do the same things as other profitable companies have done, over and over again, you will eventually earn the kind of profits that they earned.

Throughout this book, we have approached the subject of making and increasing profits over and over again. In this chapter, I will give you a series of specific causes you can initiate to achieve the results you want, the profits that you desire.

The Value-Creation Chain

Every business performs a series of functions that create or add value in some way. These steps in the value-creation chain lead to the final product or service that you sell at a price that exceeds the total costs of producing it. This excess is your profit.

To increase your profits, you must first examine every step of your own value-creation chain. Sometimes, just one change in the way you do business can lead to dramatic changes in your results.

Each part of the value-creation chain consists of an activity of some kind. You have to buy, manufacture, or produce the product or service that you are going to sell to your customers. You have to advertise, sell, and deliver what you sell. Finally, you have to ensure that your customers are so happy with their purchase that they buy again and tell their friends about you.

Analyze Every Step

You begin the process of value creation by determining exactly what your customers want, need, and will pay for. You determine the price that you can charge in order to make sales in a competitive market. You decide exactly what combination of methods you will use to market, sell, and promote your product or service. You determine the location at which you will offer your product or service. You decide upon your packaging and how every element of your business will appear to your customers.

> You begin the process of value creation by determining exactly what your customers want, need, and will pay for.

You determine your positioning and how you want to be described by customers and non-customers in your market. Finally, you select the key people who will be responsible for every step of the value-creation chain.

An improvement in any one of these areas will have an effect on your profits, either positive or negative. The starting point for doubling your profitability is to examine each one of these links and then think about things that you could do to improve financial results at each step.

Improve 10 Percent in Each Key Area

Jay Abraham, the marketing genius, teaches what he calls the *Parthenon Principle*. His insight is that, by improving your results by only 10 percent in each of the key areas of your business, the cumulative result will be a doubling of your financial results.

For years, I have personally taught the *Vital Functions Concept*. This principle is based on the fact that there are certain vital functions in the human body that are indicative of life—heart rate, blood pressure, muscle tone, brain wave activity, and so on. An absence of any of these vital functions is the clinical definition of death.

In the same sense, there are certain vital functions, sometimes referred to as Key Result Areas or Key Success Indicators, that determine the life or death of an enterprise.

Here is the point. If you decided to improve your muscle tone by exercising every day, what do you think would happen to your pulse rate and blood pressure? The answer is that, as you concentrated on improving in one area, you would automatically improve in other areas as well. If you exercised for 30-60 minutes each day, your resting pulse rate would improve, your blood pressure would decline, your muscle tone would be firmer, and your entire body would function better.

Improve in Each Key Area of Sales

You could make a plan to improve in the seven key result areas of selling: prospecting, establishing rapport and credibility, identifying needs, presenting your product or service, answering objections, closing the sale, and getting resales and referrals from your satisfied customers. As you improve in any one area, you would begin to improve in other key areas as well.

As a manager, if you became a little bit better in any one area of planning, organizing, staffing, delegating, supervising, measuring, and reporting, you would improve in each other area as well.

In generating more profits, as you get better in any one step of your value-creation chain, or in the seven P's of the marketing mix, you will find yourself automatically improving in other areas as well.

The Profit Improvement Model

The first step in increasing your profitability is to determine exactly where your profits are coming from at the present time. Earlier I mentioned that many businesses are not clear about which products and services are most profitable, after all direct and indirect expenses have been deducted. Sometimes it is a product that no one pays attention to that is the most profitable of all.

In every business there are products that are referred to as "cash cows." These are usually a staple of the business. Very often the business started and grew as the result of the success of this particular product or service. It sells consistently and predictably. Customers like it. The company produces and delivers it continuously and effortlessly. Because it is a no-hassle, problem-free product or service to sell and deliver, it is often taken for granted while the business owner is preoccupied with developing and selling new products or services.

Identify Your Core Business

Chris Zook, of the Bain Consulting Group, wrote an excellent book in 2001 called *Profit from the Core*. After examining hundreds of companies, he concluded that each business has core products and services that it is built around. These are the heartbeat of the company, what I call the "jelly in the jelly doughnut of your business."

The company is known for these products. They achieve high levels of customer satisfaction. They sell easily and consistently. The company is geared up to produce and present these products at a high level of quality. They account for the largest and most predictable profit stream of anything you do.

What Zook found was that these products often get ignored in the shuffle. The company takes them for granted. The company gets busy offering other products to other customers in other markets at other price points. In the worse case, a competitor comes along and steals away the core business while the company is looking in the other direction. You must make sure that this never happens to you.

What are your core products? What are your core services? Who are your core customers? What are your core markets? What are your core methods of marketing and advertising? What are your core sales methods? Who are your core salespeople? You must never take your eyes off your core business. This is often where the greatest improvements in profitability are possible.

Three Ways to Increase Your Sales

We have talked about these before. They never change.

The first way to increase your sales is to increase the *number* of individual sales. Companies that sell products or services that are only needed every few years or once in a lifetime, like a new furnace, have to concentrate all their business activities on increasing the number of sales.

This is true of homes, cars, motor homes, life insurance policies, wedding rings, and even appliances. Once a person has purchased one of these items, he or she is not going to be a customer in that market again for a long time.

If doubling your profitability requires that you double the number of sales of your product or service, then this becomes the central focus of your marketing, advertising, and sales strategy.

The second way to increase your sales is by making *larger* sales to each customer. Once the customer has decided to buy from you, you must think of ways to increase the size of the sale and therefore the profitability.

The good news is that, once the customer has reached the point of liking you and trusting you enough to buy from you, he or she will be open to suggestions for increasing the size of his or her purchase. Sometimes you can up-sell the customer to a more expensive item. On other occasions, you can cross-sell the customer by offering additional products or services that go along with the product or service that he or she has purchased.

Because acquiring customers can be so expensive, you can give deep discounts and bonuses to get the customer to buy something else before he or she leaves. You can cut the price on additional items by 10 percent, 25 percent, or even 50 percent to capture the add-on sale. The extra profit you earn is money that you would not have and will not have if you let the customer depart.

The third way to increase sales is by getting the customer to *buy more frequently*. If you sell a product or service that is used and consumed regularly, such as food, business services, automobile maintenance, barber and beauty services, or office stationery and supplies, the key to business growth is to capture more of the customer's business. You aim for "depth of wallet" rather than for breadth of market.

It is much easier to sell to a satisfied customer than it is to advertise, promote, and sell to a new customer. So, once you have created the customer, you must move heaven and earth to ensure that this customer buys from you again and again.

Often, all that is necessary to increase the frequency of purchase is to add something extra that costs you nothing but that customers buying from you perceive as being of high value. You can follow up with a thank-you note or a telephone call. You can offer the customers a special status with your company that gives them discounts or better service whenever they call or visit. What you can do to attract repeat business is limited only by your imagination.

You can increase the frequency at which they buy from you by offering another product or service, something that your customers purchase on a regular basis from someone else. Once you have captured the customer, you should make every effort to sell the customer as many different products and services as you can, consistent with your business model and your area of specialization.

Enter into Strategic Alliances

You can increase your sales by entering into joint ventures and strategic alliances with companies that sell non-competing products and services to the kind of customers who buy what you sell. For example, my banker for my business and personal loans recommended an accounting firm to me. The accounting firm recommended an estate lawyer, who drew up my will. The estate lawyer recommended an insurance agent, who sold me a policy to put into my life insurance trust to bypass probate and estate taxes for my family. My insurance agent recommended a restaurant that I didn't know about. The maitre d' at the restaurant recommended a florist for anniversaries and birthdays for my wife. Each business helps other businesses sell more things. Everyone benefits.

Create Host-Beneficiary Relationships

You can create *host-beneficiary relationships* in which you offer a free gift or a special bonus to the customers of another company. This free gift or bonus appears to be coming from the other company, even though it is a referral and a new customer for you.

In acquiring customers and entering into strategic alliances, joint ventures, or host-beneficiary relationships, the critical number you are considering is the *cost of acquisition*. Remember: you are in the business of "buying customers" at a price that is below the profit you earn from each sale. If you can buy your customers by advertising in various ways and you make a profit on each customer after paying your advertising costs, then you should do that more and more.

If you can buy your customers by selling something to the customers of a strategic alliance partner, either by sharing or for a commission, then you should pursue that method as well. If you can acquire customers by giving a gift to the customers of a host-beneficiary, you should go that route. Keep asking *how much* you can afford to pay to acquire a new customer. What are all the ways that you could spend that amount?

In the financial statements of a *Fortune* 500 company, there is a small footnote that says that it allocates $150 for each new customer it acquires. It spends this money on a combination of advertising and bonuses that they give to people for buying from them for the first time. Could you do something like this in your business? How much would you be willing to pay?

The Profit Curve

Each product or service that you sell yields you a specific amount of net profit. Because most companies bundle all their general expenses together, most businesspeople are not exactly sure where their largest profits are coming from.

> Most businesspeople are not exactly sure where their largest profits are coming from.

In developing your profit curve, you must first determine the *rank order* of profitability of every product or service that you sell. Which is the most profitable? Which is the least profitable? And where do all your other products or services rank in between? Most companies and businesses have no idea how to answer these questions.

You begin this process of profit analysis with the *average* sales price that you receive for an item after all discounts, defects, shrinkage, and returns. It is important that you be accurate with this number.

You then deduct 100 percent of the cost of goods sold, the exact amount that it takes to offer this product or service to your customers. You start with the cost of the product or service itself. You then deduct all advertising and marketing expenses, selling expenses, including the salaries and wages of people involved in every aspect of product or service promotion, plus the amounts that you have to pay to salespeople, including Social Security, unemployment insurance, health insurance, and transportation expenses.

Once you have deducted the total cost of goods sold, direct and indirect, from the average selling price of the product or service, you end up with your gross profit per item.

Determining Attributable Costs

You then analyze each of your administrative expenses and allocate to each product or service the exact amount that it costs to administer and account for that product or service. For example, if you have a service manager whom you pay $25,000 per year and you sell 1,000 of your product yearly, you must allocate per item $2.50 for his labor and 1/1,000th of his benefits package.

Go through every product or service that you offer and allocate the exact cost, including the percentage of rent for your facilities, the percentage of utilities costs, the percentage of management time, the percentage of every dollar of labor you spend, and even the percentage of time spent by your accountants and bookkeepers to send out invoices, collect bills, and maintain accounts.

The first time you do this exercise for a product or service you will probably be shocked. You will be surprised at the actual profit that you are making (or not) from product to product or service to service. But once you have this knowledge, you will be able to cut your costs and increase your profits.

Eliminate Low-Profit, No-Profit Items

Your first discovery will be that certain products or services take up a lot of time but are not particularly profitable. They may take up warehouse space, staff time, and costs for offices, utilities, insurance, and transportation. But you sell so few of them or at such a low profit per item that they are not worth the time and attention they take away from better-selling, higher-profit items. These are prime candidates for you to drop.

In a strategic planning exercise with a large company, I walked them through this exercise, helping them determine exactly what they actually sold, what their customers actually bought, and where their profits were coming from. After this exercise, they eliminated 80 percent of the products and services they were offering. They got back to their "core business" and dramatically increased their profitability. And this experience is not unusual.

The 80/20 Rule Prevails

No matter how you shake it down, over time, 80 percent of your profits will come from 20 percent of your activities. But the shocker is to learn that your time and administrative expenses are divided equally across the *number* of products and services you sell. They are not allocated on the basis of the profitability of these items. This means that it is probably taking you as many hours and as much time, trouble, and expense to sell low-volume, low-profit products as it does to sell your most profitable products and services.

As soon as you discontinue the low-profit 80 percent of your products and services, you also eliminate most of the expenses associated with keeping them in your lineup. Your company can often shift into higher profitability overnight. This is what turnaround artists do when they turn around a troubled company completely in just a few months. You should do the same with your business.

Use a Chainsaw

One of the famous turnaround specialists, who got into trouble with the law for overstating sales and understating expenses, was Al Dunlap. For many years, he moved from company to company. When he went into a troubled company, he was like a man with a chainsaw pruning a tree. He lopped off every low-profit, non-performing branch or activity of the company very quickly, freeing up the best people and resources to focus all their attention on the healthiest parts of the business. He earned the nickname "Chainsaw Al."

You should think of yourself as a "chainsaw" as well. You must develop the courage and decisiveness to lop off all non-performing parts of your business. The only exception would be a poor-selling product or service that you can resuscitate and save by devoting more time and talents to it. But you must be ruthlessly honest with yourself in this area or you will be "throwing good money after bad."

The Biggest Problem Is Egoism

One of the reasons why business owners are reluctant to get rid of a non-performing product or service is because it was they who *personally* thought it up. It may be a product or service that was very important when the business began. Often it is a new product or service that the owner came up with and in which he or she has invested a lot of ego. Rather than admit that it wasn't such a great idea, knowing what they know now, many business owners will take their attention away from their best-selling products and services and spend time and money promoting something that obviously has no future in the current marketplace.

> The first law of holes is "When you find yourself in one, stop digging!"

The first law of holes is "When you find yourself in one, stop digging!"

The first law of horses is "When the horse is dead, get off!"

Keep applying zero-based thinking to each product, service, and market. Keep asking yourself, "If I were not doing this now and I knew what I know now, would I start it up again today?" Get your ego out of your decision making for your business.

A Profit-Making Business

It is a general rule that you cannot increase your profits *directly*, only *indirectly*. You cannot just say that you are going to increase your profits with some specific strategy. The only thing that you can do is to improve the *variables* that ultimately determine your level of profitability. Let's look at them, one at a time.

1. Lead generation. This is the process that you use to attract interested prospects to your business. If five out of ten prospects who come into your place of business end up buying from you and you can increase the number of people coming in from 10 to 15, you can increase your sales and profits by 50 percent.

You must think about lead generation morning, noon, and night. The law of probabilities says that if you increase your number of leads, you increase your probabilities of making more and better sales.

2. Lead conversion. This the process by which you convert leads into paying customers. This is the measure of the effectiveness of your sales efforts. If you can increase your conversion rate from one out of ten to two out of ten, you can double your sales and your profits.

We have seen over and over that small changes in a single one of the seven P's of the marketing mix can lead to dramatic changes in lead conversion, such as from one out of ten to eight out of ten within 30 days. This improvement in a critical variable can be the difference between struggling in your business and becoming wealthy.

Improving your ability to sell and convert interested prospects into paying customers is one of the most important things you can do. And there is no replacement for *ongoing sales training*, both for you and for every single person who speaks to customers, either live or on the phone.

Look at every key result area in your sales process and seek ways to improve a little bit in each area. Because of the Parthenon

Principle, a small improvement in each key area can lead to an enormous improvement in overall sales results.

3. Number of transactions. This is the number of individual sales that you make to each customer that you acquire. By increasing the frequency of purchase by 10 percent, you increase your sales and profitability by the same percentage. What are some things that you could do to get your customers to buy more from you and to buy more frequently?

4. Size of transaction. This is the size of the sale and the profit that you earn from each. You should be continually looking for ways to up-sell each customer so that he or she buys more each time.

5. Profit margin per sale. This is the gross profit that you make from the sale of each product or service. By continually seeking ways to raise the price or to lower the cost of the product or service without decreasing the quality, you can inch up your profits per sale. Every

> Every dollar you raise a price, if you hold costs constant, flows straight to the bottom line as net profit.

dollar you raise a price, if you hold costs constant, flows straight to the bottom line as net profit. Every dollar you reduce expenses, if you hold sales and revenues constant, also goes straight to the bottom line as net profit.

6. Cost of customer acquisition. This is the amount that you have to pay to acquire each paying customer. You should be continually seeking creative ways to improve your advertising and promotion so that it costs you less to buy each customer. This can impact your profitability dramatically.

7. Increasing customer referrals. These are the customers who come to you as the result of referrals from your satisfied customers. Developing one or more proven *referral systems* for your business can have an inordinate impact on your sales and profitability.

It is 15 times easier to make a sale to a referral from a satisfied customer than it is to advertise, promote, cold call, and prospect to find a customer. This means that takes 1/15th of the time, energy, and expense to sell to a referral. Referral business is the very best business that you can possibly develop.

Remember the ultimate question: "On a scale of one to ten, would you refer us to others?"

Ask your customers this question regularly. If they give you a score below nine or ten, ask them what you have to do to score nine or ten from them. Then, whatever they tell you that you would need to do, find a way to do it.

Very often, customers who give you a low score will raise their score immediately if you just ask them for advice on improving their score with them. When you make the change that they've suggested as likely to cause them to refer your business to others, report back to them and tell them what you have done. Thank them for their advice and input. This will tremendously increase their loyalty and encourage them to become repeat customers as well.

8. Eliminate costly services and activities. Many companies get into a routine or rhythm of offering expensive services to their customers that they could easily discontinue with no loss of customer satisfaction.

One of our clients, a very successful mortgage broker, got into the habit of taking fresh doughnuts around to her major client companies between 8:00 and 11:00 each morning. Soon, they began to jokingly refer to her as the "Doughnut Lady."

But this goodwill activity was consuming almost half of her working day. She finally summoned up the courage to announce that, as of the first of the coming month, she would be so busy giving excellent customer service to her customers that she would no longer be able to deliver doughnuts. Her customers reacted with some disappointment, but they appreciated her commitment to customer service even more. When she stopped delivering doughnuts, her business and her income actually *doubled* because she was giving customers what they valued most of all—better service.

Look at the little services that you offer to your customers. Is there anything that you could reduce or discontinue altogether?

In our office, we had a full-time receptionist at a total cost of more than $2,000 per month. We put in a customer-friendly answering system that channels people straight to a person with one touch of the button and discontinued using the receptionist. We have never received a question or complaint about out answering system and we have saved a substantial amount of money each month. Could you do something like this?

9. Outsource business activities. You should outsource every activity in your business that your customer does not want or need or is not willing to pay for. This includes payroll, printing, janitorial services, computer service and maintenance, and other activities. Outsourcing companies that specialize in a service that is not your direct line of business can usually perform it better and for less than you can, when you add in all expenses.

> You should outsource every activity in your business that your customer does not want or need or is not willing to pay for.

Imagine taking your customers around your office and showing them everything that you do in your business. Imagine asking them, "Would you pay money for this function?" Whatever activities that your customers would not pay for are candidates for outsourcing, downsizing, or eliminating. Keep thinking about streamlining your business down to your core functions and delegating or outsourcing everything else.

10. Reduce people costs. It is estimated that each person who works for you actually costs you three to six times his or her salary. An employee to whom you pay $25,000 a year actually costs about $75,000 per year, once you have included all of his or her benefits, sick pay, offices, utilities, gasoline and other resources that the employee uses, plus the cost of your time to supervise and manage him or her.

In some companies and businesses, an employee costs as much as *six times* his or her salary. This is why companies that reduce turnover, which is very expensive, and reduce head count increase their profits immediately.

At one time, when we were starting our current business, offering a variety of products and services, our payroll grew to 22 people. As we became more efficient and streamlined, we gradually reduced our head count from 22 to 12. Surprisingly enough, our sales and profitability remained constant, but our expenses dropped like a stone. We found that all the functions that the extra people were performing could be consolidated, downsized, outsourced, or eliminated without causing our business to be less efficient or effective. Could this be true for you as well?

11. Reduce fixed costs. These are costs you incur each month whether or not you sell a single item of your product or service. These include rent, wages of full-time staff, utilities, telephone charges, pre-paid advertising, and every other regular expense you incur.

You must be continually seeking ways to reduce these costs. Whatever your fixed costs, that is the minimum that you have to reach in profits just to break even.

Not long ago, I was visiting two companies in the same business in the same city. In the morning, the owners of one company gave me a tour and showed off their brand new printing operation, including several hundred thousand dollars of sophisticated printing equipment that they had leased to publish all their brochures and workbooks. They felt that bringing all this work in-house would represent a tremendous savings for them. In the afternoon, I toured one of their competitors. They showed me an empty room where their printing facilities had been located. They told me with great pride that they had outsourced all printing to independent companies. This was going to save them tens of thousands of dollars a year, especially during those times when they had no need for printing.

Both companies were in the same industry. Both companies had the same choice, to increase or decrease fixed costs. Within a few years, the company with the world-class printing operation went bankrupt. Their fixed costs dragged them down so far that they had to shut down their business. The other company continues to thrive.

12. Increase variable costs. A variable cost is a cost that you incur only when you make a sale. This can include the costs of salespeople and sales commissions, shipping and delivery costs, overnight postage, and other forms of labor.

In our car wash business, we need several people working when business is booming. But as soon as business subsides, we immediately send home all excess staff. As a result, we have managed to turn losses into profits and dramatically streamline our operations. By lowering our variable costs as soon as sales taper off, we have created a successful business.

13. Reduce your breakeven point. This is the number of items that you must sell each month to break even or start making a profit. You remember that you determine your breakeven point by first calculating your gross profit per item and then dividing that number into your monthly fixed costs.

For example, if your monthly fixed costs are $10,000, whether you sell anything or not, and you earn $10 gross profit per item that you sell, after cost of goods sold and all selling costs, you divide $10 into $10,000 to get 1,000 units as your breakeven point for the month.

You use this breakeven point to evaluate the potential effectiveness of any advertising or any other expense that you incur to increase sales. Every expense to increase sales must be seen as an investment with an expected rate of return that is greater than the cost.

For example, if you spend $10,000 advertising and you have to sell 1,000 units to break even on your advertising, then you should have a goal of 2,000 or 3,000 units in sales in order to justify advertising. If you do not believe that there is a high probability of achieving that level of sales, you should not advertise in that medium at all.

14. Raise your prices. In many situations, you can raise your prices by 5 percent or 10 percent without experiencing any market resistance. If your products and services are of good quality and your people are friendly and helpful, a small increase in your overall prices will not drive your customers away.

Some friends of mine began publishing a magazine some years ago. They charged $18 per year for a 12-month subscription. Their subscriber base grew to 40,000, but they could never seem to make a profit. Their expenses continued to eat up all their revenues.

A business consultant friend of mine sat down and looked at their business. He determined that subscriptions to similar magazines with loyal readers were selling for $40 and $50 per year. He told them that they should immediately double their price to $36 a year. They almost had a heart attack.

But when they recovered, they announced with great trepidation that, effective January 1, the new subscription rate would be $36. Of their 40,000 subscribers, only about 5 percent canceled their subscriptions. The others gladly paid the higher amount because it was an excellent publication in a specialized field.

My publisher friends went from rags to riches overnight. Virtually 100 percent of the price increase was pure profit to them. Almost all of their costs remained the same except for a small increase for paper and printing.

On which of your products or services could you increase your prices? Are your competitors already charging higher prices for similar products and services? Which of your products and services are really popular with your customers? In those areas, a small increase in price would not have any effect on buying behavior. Announce that, effective as of the first of the coming month, your prices will be increased. Give people a little while to adjust to the price increase and then don't worry.

If you could increase your prices by 10 percent across the board, with no loss of customers, that price increase would go straight to your bottom line as profits. It could make all the difference between a marginal company and a highly profitable growth business.

15. Constraint analysis. The principle of constraints is one of the most helpful ideas you will ever learn. This principle says that, between you and any goal you have for your business, there is a constraint, a choke point or bottleneck, that determines the *speed* at which you achieve that goal.

> One breakthrough, the alleviation of one critical constraint, can enable you to double your sales and your profits.

What sets the speed at which you reach the point of doubling your profitability? What is holding you back? You must focus single-mindedly on alleviating that constraint, on removing that limiting factor. One breakthrough, the alleviation of one critical constraint, can enable you to double your sales and your profits.

Take Action on Profit Improvement

In examining all of the ways listed above for increasing your profits, directly or indirectly, which one jumps out at you first? Could you double the number of leads you are attracting? Could you double your closing rate with new prospects? Could you increase the number of sales that you make? Could you increase the size of each sale? Could you increase the frequency of each sale? Could you offer another product or service that your customers want and need? Could you enter into a joint alliance to sell to "other people's customers"?

Go through the list, one by one, and think about how you could bring about a marginal improvement in each area. Since there is always much uncertainty in any business activity, be prepared to test and measure, test and measure, test and measure until you find the method or combination of methods that works best.

Look Before You Leap

Try out your new idea on a small scale. Change your advertising or your advertising message. Change your special offers to attract customers. Change the places where you advertise. Change your prices or the discounts or bonuses that you offer to new customers. Test, test, test, measure, measure, measure.

What one change, if you made it effectively, would bring about the greatest and most predictable financial results? Whatever your answer, focus and concentrate *single-mindedly* on that particular method of profit improvement.

Study Your Financial Statements

Each month, or even weekly, sit down and focus on one key element of your business. When you examine your financial statements, focus on the biggest numbers first. Examine each of those numbers carefully. Find out what's in it. Ask questions. Why is it so high? Could we improve our operations in this area? Focus on the one thing that you could do that could bring about an immediate improvement in that particular area.

Restructure your business so that everyone is focusing all the time on increasing sales and improving profit. Measure your results daily and weekly. Make whatever changes are necessary and be prepared to react quickly to changes in the marketplace.

You must manage, motivate, and lead all of your people toward greater profits. Think about and talk about profitability all the time. Never stop until you achieve it—and then achieve it again and again.

Action Exercises

1. Identify three ways that you could increase the number of leads coming to your business, right now.

2. Identify three ways that you could increase the conversion rate of the prospects you attract through your lead generation.

3. How could you increase the size of each sale by selling more expensive products or by up-selling and cross-selling?

4. How could you decrease your costs without lowering your sales or levels of quality?

5. What strategic alliances could you enter into to sell to other people's customers and invite them to sell to yours?

6. How could you get your customers to buy from you more often?

7. What could you do to increase the number of referrals you receive from satisfied customers?

CHAPTER EIGHT

The Keys to Building a High-Profit Business

The significant problems we face cannot be solved at the same level of thinking we were at when we created them.

—*Albert Einstein*

In every industry, it seems that the top 20 percent of the businesses make 80 percent of the profits. Some companies, selling very much the same product or service in the same market, earn ten times as much as other companies. The question is always *"Why are some businesses more profitable than others?"*

We know that there is a cause-and-effect relationship between corporate activities and profitability. If you do the things that profitable companies do, you soon enjoy the kind of profits that profitable companies enjoy. To put it another way, profitability is *predictable* if you can figure out how and why it occurs in your business or your industry.

Perhaps the most important single factor in determining the profitability of a business is the quality of the *thinking* of its managers and leaders. In high-profit companies, the top people are focused on performance, results, and profitability every day, all day long.

Flexibility Is the Key

According to the Menninger Institute, the most important single quality an executive can develop is *flexibility*. In times of turbulence and rapid change, such as today, your ability to remain fluid, fast, and flexible is absolutely essential to the survival and success of your business.

The very best thinking tool for ongoing flexibility is what I call "zero-based thinking." This type of thinking requires that you continually ask yourself this question, *"Is there anything that I am doing in my business today that, knowing what I now know, I wouldn't start up again today, if I had to do it over?"*

Whenever you are experiencing stress, frustration, resistance, or poor results, whether with products or services or people, you should stop and ask yourself this question, *"Is there anything that I am doing today, that knowing what I now know, I wouldn't get into again today, if I had to do it over?"*

The inability to stop doing things that are no longer working and to discontinue people who are no longer performing is the primary reason for failure in business. On the other hand, your ability to be fast and flexible in the face of this dynamic market environment is the key to your success and the success of your business.

Challenge Your Assumptions

To put the power principles in this chapter into action, you must be open to the possibility that what you are doing today is no longer appropriate for the current situation. You must learn to make three statements, over and over again, for the rest of your business life.

First, you must learn to say, *"I was wrong!"* Fully 70 percent of your decisions will turn out to be wrong in the fullness of time. The sooner you realize that you are on the wrong road and turn back to the right road, the faster you will get to your destination of business growth and greater profitability.

Second, you must be willing to say, *"I made a mistake."* The fact is that you make mistakes all the time. There is nothing wrong with that. "Nothing ventured, nothing gained." The problems arise when you avoid admitting your mistakes and taking action to correct them.

> The problems arise when you avoid admitting your mistakes and taking action to correct them.

By the way, most people around you are aware that you have made a mistake and they are just waiting for you to have the courage and character to face up to it. The sooner you admit that you are not perfect, that you have made a mistake, and stop doing whatever it is, the faster you will move toward your goals.

The third statement that you must learn to say, over and over again, is *"I changed my mind."* The superior businessperson is always willing to change his or her mind in the face of new information that challenges the old ideas or the established way of doing things.

When you make the decision to set performance, results, and profitability as your highest goals in your business and you are willing to let go of the old ways that are not working in order to embrace the new ways that might work even better, you are on the road to building a high-profit business.

There are 21 keys to high profitability, based on more than 50 years of research with many thousands of corporations. The absence of any one of these 21 keys can, in itself, undermine your profitability and even lead to the collapse of the enterprise.

1. Develop a Clear Mission for Your Business

For you, your business, and your people to perform at a high level, you need a clear *vision* of what your business stands for and where it is going. Everyone must know the answer to the question, "Why does this business exist?"

A mission must always be defined in terms of how your business serves and benefits people. A good mission statement will contain a *method* by which the mission is to be achieved. In addition, a good mission statement will contain a *measure* so that an objective third party can assess whether or not the business is living up to its mission.

> A mission must always be defined in terms of how your business serves and benefits people.

The Fortunate 500

In a study of what Ken Blanchard called the "Fortunate 500," he and his colleagues discovered that the most profitable 20 percent of companies, in every industry, over a 30-year period, had clear written values and principles that everyone knew and committed to. In addition, the companies each had a mission statement that everyone agreed upon. Other companies may have had values and missions as well, but either they were not written down or nobody really knew what they were.

To apply for the Baldridge National Quality Award, a company must fill out a 50-page application and then invite Baldrige inspectors to study and evaluate the company for several months. The inspectors are empowered to stop any employee, at any level, and ask him or her what the values, vision, and mission of the company are. 95 percent of all the employees that the Baldrige inspectors interview must be able to answer this question without referring to notes. If the employees do not know the values, vision, and mission, the Baldrige inspectors close the file and drop the application.

Your Mission Must Be Clear

Establishing a clear mission for your company, based on the values that you believe in and refuse to compromise, is the equivalent to creating a deep concrete foundation before you begin constructing a building. The difference is that you can go back at any time and build this foundation and give your business future a more solid basis.

What are your corporate values? What is your vision for your company in the years ahead? What is your mission and how will you know that you have accomplished it? Why does your company exist? What great service is your enterprise committed to offering to the world? These are the most important questions of all in building a high-profit business.

2. Determine Exactly What Business You Are In

It is absolutely amazing how many people are not quite sure what business they are in, even though they're working in that business. The reason for this confusion is because most people define their business in terms of what their product or service *is* and what it *does*. The customer, on the other hand, cares only about what the product or service does for *him or her* to improve his or her life.

You should always define your business from the point of view of your customer. You should always define your business in terms

> You should always define your business in terms of what your products or services do for your customer.

of what your products or services do for your customer. How do your products or services affect the lives and work of your customer? What are the specific results or benefits that your customers get from your products or services? That is all they care about.

For example, at one time the railroad companies dominated cross-country transportation in the United States. But they defined their business as running railroads. In reality, their mission should have been to move people and freight over long distances in the very best way possible at the very best prices.

Because their vision of their business was limited to rail traffic, bus companies, trucking companies, shipping companies, and eventually airline companies were able to move more and more people and freight and to dominate the industry, especially in the high-profit areas of moving people and mail.

What business are you in *today*, from the point of view of your customer? What business will you be in *tomorrow* when you consider the trends in your industry? What business *should* you be in if you want to survive and thrive in this dynamic and competitive environment? What business *could* you be in if you were to make the critical changes necessary to lead your field? Remember: the very best way to predict the future is to create it. And, as strategic planner Michael Kami has said, *"Those who do not plan for the future cannot have one."*

Whatever business you are in today, it's likely going to change dramatically in the years ahead. Your job is to be a master of this change, not a victim of this change. This is a major key to profitability.

3. Determine Exactly Who Your Customer Is

This is the central question of all marketing, sales, and profitability. The ability to accurately answer this question, "Who is my customer?" is the primary determinant of the success of your business.

Define your customer as accurately and as precisely as you can. What are your customer's age, education, income, position, value base, philosophy, and background? Where exactly is your customer located, both geographically and within specific businesses or organizations? Especially, what does your customer consider value? What is your customer willing to pay for? What does your customer want or need that he or she is not now getting from someone else?

Why does your potential customer buy from your competitors? What value does your customer perceive in buying from your competitors that you do not offer? How could you offset or neutralize this perceived advantage?

Who is *not your customer,* someone who could benefit from what you sell who does not buy from you or your competitor? What would you have to do to get your non-customers to begin buying your products or services? What would they have to be convinced of?

Open Up Your Mind

Keep practicing "zero-based thinking." *If you were not now serving your current market, with your current products and services, would you start up again today?* Who are your customers likely to be tomorrow, next year, and in five years? Who could be your customers if you were to change your product or service offerings? Who should be your customers if you want to be a high-profit business in the future?

Finally, what changes do you need to make in your business to be able to attract and keep the high-profit customers of tomorrow? This is perhaps the most important question that you ask and answer in building and maintaining a high-profit business.

4. Develop Competitive Advantage—or Don't Compete

Your business depends for its very survival on your ability to develop and maintain a meaningful competitive advantage of some kind. What is it that your company does really well? Where do you perform at a high level? What is the area of excellence of your key products or services?

Your competitive advantage is the aspect of your product or service that makes you *superior* in a meaningful way to your competitors. Your area of competitive advantage is always defined in terms of what your customer wants, needs, and is willing to pay for.

Every company that survives and thrives has a specific and valued competitive advantage that customers recognize and appreciate. Every company that gets into trouble has either lost its competitive advantage or never had one.

Your ability to develop, maintain, and protect your competitive advantage is the absolutely indispensable requirement for growing your business and increasing your profitability.

Think About the Future

And since your market is changing so rapidly, you must continually ask, "What will my competitive advantage be tomorrow, based on the trends in my industry?" What should your competitive advantage be in the future if you want to be in the top 10 percent of your industry? What could your competitive advantage be if you were to make the necessary changes in your product and service offerings?

Jack Welch of General Electric is famous for his belief that you must be either number one or number two in your industry or you must get out and concentrate your resources where becoming number one or two is possible. He says, "If you don't have competitive advantage, don't compete!"

The major competitive advantages today are "faster, better, cheaper," combined with superb and timely customer service. The fastest-growing and most profitable companies offer high-quality products and services and they offer them quickly. In addition, they give excellent customer service, which they continually improve. As the result, they become the leaders in their industries. This should be your goal as well.

5. Take a Long-Term View of Your Business

Your ability to think intelligently about your business today and about your business in the future can have a major impact on the growth and profitability of your enterprise. All top business owners and executives are long-term thinkers. They project forward five years and think about *where* they want to be and *what* they will have to be doing at that time in order to achieve those goals.

Some of the best work on strategic planning in recent years has been done by Gary Hamel and C.K. Prahalad. Their contribution to business thinking centers on their idea that, in order to lead your field in the future, you may have to develop specific *core competencies* that you probably do not have today. The key to long-term strategic thinking is to identify the core competencies you will require and then begin immediately to either develop or acquire those core competencies so that you will be strongly positioned for the competitive environment of the future. And if you do not, you can be sure that your competitors will do so, sooner or later.

Peter Drucker said that he never makes *predictions.* He merely looks at what is going on already and identifies the likely consequences in the years ahead. You should do the same.

What are the *trends* in your business? Where is your market going? How is your market changing with regard to people, technology, products, services, finances, and competition? What new capabilities and skills will you need three to five years from now to be at the top of your field? What steps will you have to take today to begin developing those skills and abilities?

Your responsibility is to regularly stand back, think about the future, and then begin taking steps in the *short term* to guarantee that you will create the business and achieve the profitability that you desire in the *long term.* This ability to think long term has never been more important or more valuable than now.

6. Develop a Clear Sense of Direction

You have heard it said that, when you are up to your you-know-what in alligators, it's hard to remember that you came here to drain the swamp. This is an apt description of many businesses today.

Because of the turbulence and rapid change in today's marketplace, most business owners and managers have been reduced to *operating* day by day, almost like firefighters. They are totally preoccupied with short-term problems and the need to get short-term sales and profits. They intend to spend more time thinking and planning for the future, but they don't ever seem to get around to it.

> **P**erhaps your most important responsibility to your people is to give them a clear sense of direction in their work.

But this is not for you. You need to set clear targets for yourself and for every part of your business. In fact, perhaps your most important responsibility to your people is to give them a clear sense of direction in their work. According to psychologists, the greatest single demotivator in the world of work is *not knowing what's expected.*

Practice the GOSPA Formula

There is a simple five-part formula for setting goals and strategic planning that you can use for the rest of your career. It is called the *GOSPA Formula.* Here is how it works.

"G" is for *goals*. A goal is a specific target or place where you want to be at the end of a specific period. For example, your goal could be a certain volume of sales or a certain dollar level of profitability at the end of the year.

"O" is for *objectives*. These are the sub-goals that you must achieve in order to achieve your long-term goals. If your one-year goal is a certain dollar level of profitability, your objectives could be targets in the areas of sales, distribution, manufacturing, cost control, staff development, technology installation, and so on.

"S" is for *strategies*. Your strategy is the method that you will use to achieve the particular objective on the way to your goal. For example, with regard to sales, your strategy could be to build an internal sales force or to outsource all selling to a professional sales organization. And a sales strategy could consist of sub-strategies.

"P" is for *priorities*. What are the things that you must do *first* and what are the things that you must do *second*? Which items are more important and which items are less important?

"A" is for *activities*. These are the specific daily functions that are clearly delegated to specific individuals with standards of performance and deadlines.

If you have thought through this process completely, each activity will be determined by the current priorities. Achieving the priorities will lead to achieving the strategy. When you carry out your strategy, you will achieve your objectives; at the end of the time period, you will have reached your goal of a specific level of profitability.

One of the primary qualities of executives in high-profit businesses is that they think and act strategically at all times. They are always playing down the board. They are always thinking about the future and about the actions they can take to make their desired future a reality.

7. Focus on High-Profit Activities

One of the keys to high profitability in your business is to focus more and more time and energy on producing and delivering the products and services that yield the highest possible profit to your organization.

One of the reasons for failure in business is that the company diversifies too much, spreads its energies and resources over too many products, and ends up producing too many things that contribute only marginally to the bottom line. You know exactly what I mean.

Too many companies are offering too many products and services, at too many price points, to too many different markets, in too many different ways. The proper strategy is to focus your resources on those specific areas where you can make the greatest profits.

Make a list of every product or service you offer. Gather all of the costs that are involved in bringing that product or service to the market. Examine the level of sales volume of that product. Then determine exactly how much profit you make for each one of those products or services.

You will find that, if you have a dozen products and services, one of them is yielding more profit that any of the others. You will find that 20 percent of your products or services are yielding 80 percent of your total profits. You will also find that the 80 percent of products and services that are giving you only 20 percent of the profits are probably consuming 80 percent of your costs of operation. When you do the analysis, the results are likely to surprise you, maybe even shock you!

> You will find that, if you have a dozen products and services, one of them is yielding more profit that any of the others.

Then, because you are a long-term thinker, you should ask, "What are going to be the high-profit products or services of tomorrow? What are the trends? What will we have to do today to be in a position to dominate the high-profit markets of the future?" This is a major key to profitability.

8. Set Clear Performance Targets

Remember: what gets *measured* gets done. You need clear performance targets, targets that are quantifiable and measurable. You can't hit a target that you can't see. It is absolutely amazing how many people in every organization have no real idea how to measure their performance. This is a major source of demoralization and unhappiness.

Humans have a subconscious "urge to complete." In order to be happy, people need to have a beginning, a middle, and an end to every task.

One of your most important jobs as a business owner is to set standards of performance for every task and every activity. You are responsible for establishing clear lines of responsibility, schedules, and deadlines for specific jobs. And then your job is to make sure that all people involved do what they are responsible for doing and meet the set standard according to the schedule.

In high-performance, high-profit organizations, all the people know exactly what they are expected to do, when they are expected to do it, and how their performance will be measured. All rewards and bonuses are tied into clear, measurable performance. This leads to high levels of motivation, commitment, and enthusiasm among all who are working to achieve clear goals.

9. Manage by Wandering Around

The best executives spend 75 percent of their time walking around and interacting with their staff. This enables them to get accurate and timely feedback about what is going on, long before it ever appears on a report or monthly statement.

Lou Gerstner turned IBM around within one year by freeing up the sales managers from paperwork and sending them out into the field with their salespeople to visit customers and make sales. Since it is only revenue growth that leads to higher profits, within one year IBM had turned around completely.

Have a staff meeting once a week. Discuss what everybody is doing and how it is going. Meet with your individual staff members regularly, daily if possible. Keep your door open and keep the flow of communication going. In this way, you will know everything that is going on and you will be in a position to move quickly whenever quick action on your part is advisable or necessary. This is a major key to growth and profitability.

10. Develop An Obsession with Customer Service

There is a direct relationship between the philosophy of the business owner in terms of customers and the way the staff treats the customers. In the best companies, the key people look upon the customers as special and important in every way. This philosophy or attitude permeates the entire organization.

Today, we are in the *age of the customer* as never before. Today, customers will walk away from us, after being with us for years, if someone else will serve them better or cheaper. Every day, the bar on customer service is being raised by our competitors and we have to continue to jump higher just to keep our place in the lineup.

Four Levels of Customer Service

There are four levels of customer service that you can attain in your business.

The first level is simply to *meet* expectations. This is the minimum for survival. If all you do today is *meet* the expectations of your customers, you are living on borrowed time.

The second level of customer service is to *exceed* expectations. Your ability to exceed expectations will keep you in the market for a little while longer, but you are a sitting duck for a competitor who can do better, who can exceed your level of service.

The third level of customer service is to *delight* your customers, by doing things for them, faster, better, and more cheerfully than they could have possibly expected. You achieve this level when your customers leave you with smiles on their faces, determined to come back.

The fourth level of customer service is to *amaze* your customers, to do things for them that so surprise them that they not only come back, but also tell others about their experiences.

It is the individuals and organizations that delight and amaze their customers that *own* the markets of the future. Your job is to set these standards within your organization. Your job is to continually emphasize how important your customers are and both encourage and reward every person who demonstrates this attitude in dealing with customers. This is essential to growth and profitability.

11. Put a Strong Emphasis on Sales and Marketing

The key to *high profitability* is *high sales*. The key to *business success* is *high sales*. The key to *high stock prices* and a *great future* for yourself and others is *high sales*. On the other hand, the primary reason for *business failure* is *low sales*. The primary cause of stress, frustration, firings, takeovers, and bankruptcies is *low sales*.

In the best companies, the sales and marketing people are the most respected. They are paid well and promoted faster. In the best companies, the entire company thinks and talks about sales, customers, and revenue generation all the time, all day long.

The keys to great sales are simple.

First, hire well. The best companies have the best salespeople—and they have the best salespeople because they hire them very carefully.

Second, train them thoroughly. The best and most profitable companies have the most advanced sales training programs. The worst companies do no sales training at all.

Third, manage them professionally. A good sales and marketing team is like a crack military organization. It has great officers and great leadership. Your ability to build a team of world-class sales professionals is the key to business and sales growth and to profitability, without which nothing else will work.

12. Appoint and Support Strong, Effective Key Executives

Leadership makes the critical difference in every organization. Dozens of chief executive officers are fired from top companies every year. In every case, the ultimate reason given for the firing was "failure to perform." And the major reason these senior executives have failed to perform is because they appointed weak managers and executives under them and then they did not have the courage to replace them when they did a poor job and failed to get the results expected of them.

There is nothing that brings about a more rapid change in the fortunes of a business than to change the key people in charge of getting results. The best people are future-oriented, goal-oriented, result-oriented, solution-oriented, and action-oriented. Top people have high levels of energy. They are in continual motion. They take high levels of initiative and are always looking for ways to go the extra mile, to exceed expectations, to do more than anyone expects.

The fastest way for you to push to the front in your business is for you to do more than you are paid to do, for you to ask for or take on additional responsibility and then get more and better results than anyone expected. A company can achieve high profits only if it has competent people in every key position. The absence of just one key person in one key position can be enough to cause the company to underperform or even fail.

13. Staff Well at All Levels

The best companies have the best people. The second-best companies have the second-best people. The third-best companies are on their way out of business. Your ability to select good people and then to manage them well is the critical determinant of the success of your business. People are everything.

95 percent of your success will be determined by the people you hire for key positions. 95 percent of your problems will come from having put the wrong people in the wrong positions. The rule is for you to "hire slow and fire fast." Interview people at least three times and check their references carefully. Take your time. Be patient. And once you have hired someone, appoint a person to work with your new hire full time until he or she feels comfortable with the job.

Fortunately, you can learn how to interview and hire good people. It is a key skill, a key result area. Your ability to pick excellent people can be the major factor in your success as an executive.

14. Teach, Train, and Develop Your People

The rule is that you cannot expect people to perform at high levels unless you have thoroughly *trained* them to perform at those levels. The most profitable businesses in America spend the most on training their people. The companies that are marginal spend little or nothing on training.

Xerox conducted a study on the effectiveness of its training programs recently. They found that they are getting $22 back to the bottom line for every dollar they invest in training their people. IBM found that they are getting $26 back to the bottom line for every dollar they invest in their people. And Motorola found that they are getting $33 back for every dollar they invest in their people.

Resolve today to turn your company into a *learning organization*. The top 20 percent of companies in America, according to the American Society for Training and Development, spend three percent or more of their gross revenues on training the people who are expected to generate and process those revenues. How does this compare with the amount that your company spends?

The president of a *Fortune* 500 company said recently, *"Our only source of sustainable competitive advantage is our ability to learn and apply new ideas faster than our competition."* This should be your philosophy as well.

15. Develop a Caring Work Environment

You've heard it said, *"They don't care how much you know until they know how much you care."* Not only are the people the most important asset of your business, but people are also completely emotional. People perform to the degree to which they feel that their superiors care about them as individuals.

In today's tight labor markets, your ability to attract and keep good people is vital to your success. And the better your people, the more they expect to be treated with kindness, courtesy, respect, and openness.

> The better your people, the more they expect to be treated with kindness, courtesy, respect, and openness.

Treat your staff as though they were members of your own family. Treat them as though they were volunteers who were working without pay and who could withhold their services at any time. Treat them as though they have just received a job offer from another company at a higher salary. Treat them as if your whole business and future depends on them—because it does.

16. Develop and Maintain High Levels of Commitment

Hire and keep only people who are willing to put their whole hearts into the job and into making your business successful.

Your very best people will always be those with the highest level of personal commitment to you and to getting results. Your biggest problems will always come from people who are uncommitted in some way, for some reason.

The average person works at less than 50 percent of capacity. Many of them complain, criticize, and gossip regularly. This form of negativity undermines all your best efforts to build a top team.

Ask yourself, based on your experience, *"Is there anybody working for me today that, knowing what I now know, I wouldn't hire back again today, if I had to do it over?"*

Your job as the executive is to create and maintain harmony among your team members. And the measure of the degree of harmony is how much people *laugh* together at work. A happy, healthy work environment is one where people laugh a lot, joke a lot, smile a lot, and are generally happy. And one negative, uncommitted, complaining person can disrupt an entire business.

More and more companies today hire on the basis of *attitude and personality.* People can learn the skills and abilities, but attitude and personality are largely fixed. Look for positive people and then create an environment where they feel terrific about themselves.

17. Run the Business Like a Turnaround

Very often when a large business gets into serious financial trouble, it brings in a team of turnaround artists. These people take firm control of every expenditure in the company and begin operating as if the company were on the verge of financial collapse.

You should do the same. Run a tight ship. Be deadly serious about costs and expenses. Pay very close attention to every dollar that flows in and out of the company. Cut out, cut back, and eliminate all nonessential expenditures regularly.

Set a standard for *frugality*, for careful use of funds. Lead by example. Help everyone in the company to be extremely sensitive to the impact of expenditures on the bottom line and on the future success of the enterprise.

All good companies are thoughtful and careful about money. As a result, they make far better buying and selling decisions and turn out to be more profitable in the long term.

18. Form Strategic Alliances at All Levels

Strategic alliances are essential for the long-term health and prosperity of your company. Business is so complex today that the only way you can succeed is by allying with other business enterprises, in other areas, so that you can all perform at your very best.

> Form strategic alliances with your suppliers and work together with them to improve quality, delivery times, and inventory levels.

Form strategic alliances with your suppliers and work together with them to improve quality, delivery times, and inventory levels. Form strategic alliances with your customers so that they see you and your business as *partners*, as an essential part of their business. Form strategic alliances with the businesses that offer products and services to your customers but that do not compete directly with your business.

The key to high profitability is to simplify your operations and specialize on high-value, high-profit activities. This requires that you downsize, outsource, or even eliminate those activities that are not absolutely essential for the success of your business. The most successful companies are those who have built a network of strategic alliances all around them, at all levels. These alliance partners help them to operate at the highest levels of efficiency and, in turn, they help their alliance partners in every way possible.

19. Provide Outstanding Quality, Performance, and Service

Your most important asset as a company is your *reputation* in the marketplace. It is how you are known to your customers. Your most valuable asset is the way in which your customers think about you, talk about you, and describe you to others when you are not there.

To achieve high profitability, you should think through and decide clearly how you want to be seen and thought about in the marketplace. You must then organize and reorganize every part of your business so that you create the impression that is most conducive to high levels of repeat sales and maximum profitability of your most important products and services.

A reputation for *quality* in everything you do will help you more than a reputation for any other single thing in selling more and more of your products and services to more and more customers. Never relax your striving for ever higher levels of quality. Never become complacent with success. Remember: "Good enough seldom is."

A great rule for business success is this: "Do only those things that you can do in an *excellent* fashion." If you cannot do it in an excellent fashion, better than any of your competitors, and you do not have the resources to bring your standards up to that level, you should not be in that area of business at all.

Demand the best—of yourself, of your people, and of your products and services. Be relentless in your pursuit of quality. Tell everyone around you that product and service quality are absolutely essential. Make any sacrifice, pay any price, and even take any loss, if necessary, to keep up your high standards. This will add to your profitability as much as or more than any other single factor.

20. Dedicate Resources to Research and Development

Successful companies spend 10 percent or more of their gross revenues on research and development activities aimed at bringing new products and services to the market. 3M aims to have 20 percent of its revenues each year coming from new products developed within the last five years.

The fastest-growing companies in America, especially high-tech companies, invest hundreds of millions and even billions of dollars in research and development. They work at a frantic pace. They know that their competitors, in every area, are also willing to invest the same sums to develop an edge in the industry.

Think things through and then be willing to take intelligent risks to develop the products and services of tomorrow. Fully 80 percent of everything that everyone is consuming today will be obsolete within five years. This means that fully 80 percent of all products and services being consumed in five years do not even exist today.

Many companies have found, by vigorously pursuing research and development activities, that they can enter into brand new markets with brand new products and services that enable them to become giants in their industries. And this is possible only with a senior executive focus, combined with substantial budgets, on developing the products and services of tomorrow.

What Is Your Next Miracle?

Here is a good exercise. Assume that your primary source of sales and profits today, your main product or service, will be obsolete and out of the market within three to five years. What will be your next product or service? What are you developing right now for the future to replace your top-selling products of today?

Every year, leading companies are pushed aside by aggressive, brash, smaller competitors that were willing to channel large sums into R & D and that have managed to jump to the lead position in the industry. You remember Satchel Paige, the baseball player who once said, "Don't look back; something might be gaining on you."

In today's dynamic marketplace, your competitors are racing to get ahead of you, 24 hours a day. You have to run twice as fast just to stay where you are. To get ahead, you have to run even faster.

21. Create Great Morale in your Organization

There was a study completed and a book written in 1988 by Robert Levering entitled *A Great Place to Work*. In this study, they interviewed many thousands of employees to ask them what constituted a great job and a great company. Here are the answers.

First, the work was challenging and interesting.

Second, there was a high level of trust and support, which was demonstrated by the fact that the managers did not criticize or fire people for making mistakes. This was an extremely important part of the definition of a great place to work.

Third, people felt that they were "in the know." The company had wide open communications, in all directions, and employees felt as if they were active participants and "insiders" in everything that was going on.

Fourth, in a great place to work, employees felt as if their boss cared about them each as a person rather than just as an employee. The boss treated each person with consideration, courtesy, and kindness on a regular basis.

Fifth, the happiest employees said that they knew exactly what they were supposed to do, and to what standard, and by what time.

Finally, in a great place to work, people felt that there were opportunities for advancement based on hard work and excellent performance.

Your job is to create a place where people feel terrific about themselves. Your job is to create a high-energy environment where people are enthusiastic about coming to work. Your job is to be a positive, supportive, and at the same time result-oriented boss. These are the ingredients necessary to create a great morale, high productivity, high levels of creativity, and loyal employees.

Summary

Let me summarize this chapter with a few key points. Perhaps the most important is that the real key to business success is *leadership*. The key to leadership is for you to accept 100 percent responsibility for results, with no excuses, no complaining, and no blaming of other people.

The most important thing a leader can do is to *lead by example*. Be a role model for the people around you. Continually ask yourself this question, *"What kind of a company would this company be, if everyone in it were just like me?"*

Whatever your answer to that question, make sure that, if everyone behaved the way you did, this would be a great place to work.

Be open to new ideas, at all times. Be willing to try something new and different with no guarantees. Read, learn, discuss, and seek good ideas everywhere. Invite and encourage suggestions and input from everyone.

Finally, become intensely action-oriented. All successful businesspeople and profitable companies are on what is called a "continuous offensive." They are always trying new things, always moving forward. They have a sense of urgency and a bias for action.

Resolve today to build an exciting, happy, high-energy, high-profit company and then do what thousands of other companies have done to achieve this goal. Whatever other companies have done, you can do as well—and probably better. There are no limits except the limits you place on yourself.

Action Exercises

1. Develop a company mission statement that explains to everyone why you are in business, what you intend to accomplish for your customers, and how you will measure success.

2. Identify your ideal customer and then determine exactly what you will have to do to attract and keep more of these customers.

3. Determine your special area of competitive advantage, what you offer that makes you superior to any of your competitors. What is it today? What should it be? What could it be?

4. Write a description of the perfect person you need to attract to fill a key position in your business. Why would this person want to work for you?

5. Analyze and decide upon the 20 percent of your products, services, and activities that contribute 80 percent of your profits. Then focus on them above all others.

6. What are the three most important contributions that you can make personally to the growth and profitability of your business?

7. Practice zero-based thinking on everything. Is there anything you are doing today, knowing what you now know, that you wouldn't get into again today if you had it to do over?

CHAPTER NINE

Balancing Your Work and Personal Life

The return from your work must be the satisfaction which that work brings you and the world's need of that work. With this, life is heaven, or as near heaven as you can get.

—*W.E.B. DuBois*

---

hat do you want to be when you grow up? What do you *really* want to be?

That may sound like a very simple if not silly question, but it goes right to the heart of the most important things you'll ever deal with. It's amazing how many of us put off our real lives until something else happens. Lawrence Durrell, author of *The Alexandria Quartet*, wrote, *"I do not write for those who have never asked themselves this question, 'At what point does real life begin?'"*

The most important indicator that you have made the decision that real life has already begun is your commitment to achieving and maintaining *balance* in every part of your life. In this final chapter of *The Road to Wealth*, I want to share with you some ideas with regard to balance as it affects all areas of your life, including your family.

Balance Is Essential for Happiness

In this sense, the words "balance" and "alignment" mean very much the same thing. If the wheels of your car are out of alignment, they will start to wobble and shake and your entire car will vibrate. If the imbalance goes on for too long, the wobbling will wear down the bearings and the axles and a wheel might even fall off, causing a serious accident.

In your life, the same principle applies. If your life is out of balance or out of alignment for very long, your relationships and your work begin to suffer.

> If your life is out of balance or out of alignment for very long, your relationships and your work begin to suffer.

Just as your car begins to vibrate and your wheels begin to wobble, your life begins to make you stressed, anxious, and frustrated.

Your overall goal should be to be *happy*. It should be to be calm, confident, and relaxed and to feel in complete control of every aspect of your life. Just as your car runs more smoothly and requires less energy to go faster and farther when your wheels are in perfect alignment, you perform better in every area of your life when your thoughts, feelings, emotions, goals, and values are in alignment as well.

Nature Demands Balance

Nature demands balance in all things. You see balance all around you, from the most distant stars in the universe right down to the individual cells of your body. Each of your billions of cells contains hundreds of chemicals, each of which is carefully regulated and kept in balance by your autonomic nervous system to ensure your health and longevity. An imbalance leads to illness and disease.

The wonderful thing is that balance is the norm in your life. Your body has a natural bias toward health and energy. It is built to last for a hundred years and to perform smoothly and efficiently for most of that time. It is only improper maintenance and incorrect operation that, in most cases, cause your body to get out of balance and lead you into disease and pain, rather than ease and pleasure.

Emotionally, you also have a natural bias toward happiness and satisfaction. In fact, you have a natural barometer inside of you that tells you when you are doing the things that are just right for your unique personality and temperament. This is your *inner voice*, your intuition, and it is focused on helping you to achieve peace of mind.

Whenever you feel at peace with yourself and the world around you, you know that you are doing the very things that you are meant to do and that your inner and outer worlds are properly balanced and in alignment with each other.

The Law of Correspondence

There is a law of correspondence that has been written about throughout all the ages. It says simply that your outer world will be a reflection of your inner world. This law says that almost everything that happens to you on the *outside* occurs as the result of something that is happening to you on the *inside*.

> Your relationships, your attitude, the amount of money you make, and your physical health are largely determined by the way you think and feel and respond to the world around you.

Your relationships, your attitude, the amount of money you make, and your physical health are largely determined by the way you think and feel and respond to the world around you. In this sense, you are very much responsible for the outer aspects of your life because you control the inner attitudes of your mind.

This law of correspondence is unbreakable and unavoidable, but it is a two-edged sword. Just as it explains why things go right in your life, it also points the finger clearly at you when things go wrong. Your chief responsibility in achieving balance is to ensure that your inner world is consistent with what you want to enjoy and experience in your outer world. And this is completely up to you.

Happiness Is the True Measure

Your normal, natural, healthy state of being in life is to experience joy and laughter in most of what you do. The measure of how together you are as an individual is easily taken by looking at how often you *laugh* at what is going on around you. In fact, the percentage of time you have a *positive mental attitude* toward yourself and toward the normal ups and downs of your life is a measure of your degree of mental health.

People who are pessimistic and negative and who see the dark side of the things that happen to them are suffering from a mild but nevertheless debilitating form of mental illness. If a person is negative for too long, negativity becomes a habitual pattern of thought and action. The individual soon sees the whole world through lenses tinged with pessimism and unhappiness, skepticism and suspicion.

You can maintain better levels of balance by developing the habit of *looking for the good* in people and situations around you. By disciplining yourself to look for the valuable lesson in each difficulty that you face, you take full control of your conscious mind. You see the world in a more optimistic and constructive way. In seeing your world the way you want it to be, you find your whole world coming more and more into balance with the kind of life you want to live.

Two Elements of Balance

There are two major areas of balance you need to be concerned with daily—the *physical* and the *emotional*. You need to adjust your behaviors in such a way that you enjoy high levels of physical health and energy most of the time. Even the richest person in the world is at a tremendous disadvantage if his or her health suffers. You must guard your health like something sacred. You should think from the time you get up in the morning to the time you go to bed at night about the various things you can do to ensure that you live a long, healthy life. You should aim to be free from the diseases and the debilitating illnesses that keep so many people from enjoying life.

Some years ago, the Alameda Health Study was conducted on 8,000 men over a period of 20 years. The purpose of the study was to determine what physical habits they had that caused some of them to live longer or to die earlier than their peers. This study discovered that there were *seven* common habits practiced regularly by people who were the healthiest, lived the longest, and had the fewest sick days.

Seven Steps to a Longer Life

The first of these seven habits is to *eat regularly*. Researchers found that people who ate irregularly, at different times and in different amounts throughout the day, were far more likely to be constipated, be fatigued, and have physical ailments than were those who ate regularly.

The second habit is to *eat lightly*. We know today that foods high in fat, sugar, and salt are bad for us. The more you tilt your diet toward fruits, vegetables, whole grains, and lean sources of proteins, plus lots of water, the better you will feel, the deeper you will sleep, and the more energy and vitality you will have.

The third habit, which also had to do with diet, is *no snacking between meals*. When you snack between meals, the introduction of new food interrupts the ongoing digestive process and causes drowsiness, constipation, and improper digestion.

The fourth habit for longevity is *not smoking*. Smoking is so detrimental to the entire human system that it alone causes more illnesses than all other environmental or hereditary factors put together. Researchers have identified at least 32 forms of disease, including a variety of cancers, that are

> **R**esearchers have identified at least 32 forms of disease, including a variety of cancers, that are caused or aggravated in some way by smoking.

caused or aggravated in some way by smoking. The very act of quitting smoking can do more to improve a person's overall health than any other single change in health habits.

The fifth habit identified in the Alameda Study is *moderate or no consumption of alcohol*. This is a fairly narrow range that suggests not more than one or two drinks per day; fewer is better. The primary cause of premature death prior to the age of 40 is automobile accidents. As many as 50 percent of automobile accidents are alcohol-related. Cutting down or eliminating alcohol can therefore contribute significantly toward ensuring that you live a long life.

The sixth habit for longevity is *sleeping seven to eight hours* every night. Keeping properly rested is one of the most important things you can do. If you allow yourself to become overtired, your immune system begins to break down. As a result, you become susceptible to a variety of illnesses, including colds, flu, and even pneumonia. Getting regular rest is one of the most important parts of keeping your physical life in balance.

The seventh health habit identified in the Alameda Study was *regular exercise*. The rule with regard to your body is "If you don't use it, you lose it." Every joint in your body is meant to be fully articulated every day. Regular exercise, even moderate, can help you to feel better, digest better, sleep better, and be a happier and more positive person.

Even More Ways to Live Longer

The life insurance industry has identified two additional positive health habits since the Alameda Study was conducted. The first is wearing *seat belts* in your car to reduce the possibility of harm in a crash. Second is *deep breathing* each day to improve your digestion and increase the flow of oxygen to your brain. Deep breathing also causes you to relax, enabling you to drop into a state of alpha on a regular basis.

> **D**eep breathing also causes you to relax, enabling you to drop into a state of alpha on a regular basis.

In fact, one of the very best ways to engage in the process of "centering," calming your mind, is to take a few moments prior to any event of importance and to breathe deeply six or seven times. Deep breathing causes you to relax and makes you feel more confident. It causes you to feel more in control of yourself and the situation. It brings your inner world into better alignment with what is going on around you.

Whenever you face a stressful situation, such as a sales call or a business presentation, you can better prepare to deal with it by taking a few moments to breathe deeply before you say or do anything. When you prepare yourself in this way, your words and actions will be better considered and more effective than if you had just reacted to the situation. You will feel more in balance. And the more you act as though you are in balance, the more it becomes a habit for you to behave in a more balanced way.

Vince Lombardi once said, "Fatigue makes cowards of us all." When you are physically out of balance for any reason, when you're tired or you've eaten too much or too much of the wrong foods, it affects your emotions, your level of energy, and your reactions to situations around you. When you are in excellent health, well rested, properly exercised, and have eaten the right foods, you're much more likely to perform at your best.

Maintain a Healthy Emotional Life

The second area of balance that is important to you is in your emotional life. How you feel emotionally has a dramatic impact on your physical body. The whole field of psychosomatic medicine deals with the impact of "psycho" (the mind) on "soma" (the body) and shows that 80 to 90 percent of physical illnesses are mentally and emotionally induced.

How can you tell if you are out of balance emotionally? It's easy. Just listen to your body and your emotions.

Like a doctor, take a stethoscope to your life and listen intently to how you feel about how things are going on around you. When you are in balance, you feel calm, confident, relaxed, poised, and at peace with yourself and life. When you are out of balance, you feel unhappy, stressed, anxious, angry, resentful, negative, pessimistic, and depressed.

In each area of your life, you will have a different set of feelings. In some parts of your life, you will be perfectly happy. In other parts of your life, you will feel uneasy, tense, and sometimes frustrated. Your job is to go through your life, like going through your closet to throw out old clothes, and take the time to develop a strategy to deal with each part of your life that is detracting from your happiness.

The normal and natural state of your body and your life is that of joy and laughter. People who have fully integrated personalities experience a sense of pleasure and joy at the things that happen in their lives. They have an optimistic attitude toward what is going on around them. They see the good points in each person and situation they deal with. Like Will Rogers, they say, "I never met man (or woman) I didn't like."

Your Inner Program

The most important breakthrough in understanding human nature in the 20th century was the discovery of the *self-concept*.

Your self-concept is the master program of your personal computer. It's made up of all the ideas, experiences, decisions, emotions, knowledge, and beliefs that you've acquired from infancy and possibly from even before that. Your self-concept serves as the *operating instructions* for your mental computer. You always behave on the outside in a manner consistent with your self-concept on the inside.

Because of the role of your self-concept, you cannot change anything in your outer world permanently until and unless you first change the way you think. You have to change your mind about yourself to change your reality.

Your Multiple Self-Concepts

You have several *mini self-concepts.* You have a self-concept for the kind of person you are, for your personality, your attitude, and your values. You have a self-concept for the kind of life you lead, for your income, your home, your car, and the type of work that you do. You have a self-concept for your health and your weight and your level of fitness. You have a self-concept for how well you perform in any athletic endeavor. You have a self-concept that governs your level of creativity, intelligence, sense of humor, memory, ability to speak to a public audience, and level of competence in everything else that you do. And you always act on the outside consistent with your self-concept, your inner programming.

To get your life more into balance, you must carefully examine your inner world. You must hold it up, like a picture frame, to your outer world and compare both worlds. You must find where there is incongruence between the inner and outer that might be causing you to perform poorly or to be unhappy and frustrated.

Your self-concept is made up of three parts—your *self-ideal,* your *self-image,* and your *self-esteem.*

Your Self-Ideal

Your self-ideal is the person that you would most like to be. This is a composite of the values that you feel are the highest you could have and live by. Your self-ideal is shaped by the qualities that you most admire in yourself and in other people. Sometimes, you can clarify your self-ideal by asking yourself what you would look like and how others would describe you if you became the finest person you could ever become.

I often encourage people in my seminars to write out a *personal mission statement* based on their values, vision, mission, and purpose in life. I then ask them to write out a *eulogy*, a description of the person they became over the course of their lifetime that would be read at their funeral.

Here is another exercise. Imagine that you have died and that you had left instructions for people to write *two words* describing you on your headstone. How would you like most to be remembered? What two descriptive adjectives would you want people to apply to you?

Determine Your True Values

Values clarification and values definition are something that very few people ever engage in. But all superior men and women are very clear about what they stand for. You need to be clear as well. You need to think through not only your values, but also the order in which you would place them.

The rule is that a *higher-order value* always takes precedence over a lower-order value, especially when a person is under pressure. For example, if you say that your three top values are your family, your health, and your career, this order means that you would always choose your family over your health and career, and your family and health over your career.

But, imagine another person with the same values, in a different order. This other person also values family, health, and career, but he puts them in the sequence of career, family, and health. This means that he would choose his career over his family, and his career and family over his health.

Let me ask you, would there be a *difference* between the first person and the second person? Would there be a difference between the person who says, "My family comes before my health and my career" and the person who says, "My career comes before my health and my family"?

And the answer is "Of course!" There would be an enormous difference. Just the change in the ordering of the values would make these people into two totally different personalities.

They would be so different that you would instantly recognize either one of them in a few moments of conversation. The first person would have values that would lead to a happy life, while the second person would have values that would lead to continued frustration, unhappiness, and imbalance.

> Once you have thought through your values, you then look at your actions and your behaviors and ask yourself, "How do my behaviors align with my values?"

Once you have thought through your values, you then look at your actions and your behaviors and ask yourself, "How do my behaviors align with my values?" You can tell what you truly believe only by looking at what you do when you are *forced to choose.* You are always free to choose your actions. Whenever you make a choice, you are making a value statement for the entire world to see.

Live Congruent with Your Values

Many people find that, although they pay lip service to their family, their relationships, and their health, they're very quick to sacrifice them or to relegate them to secondary importance when a demand of work or an opportunity for material success arises. However, if your goals and activities are not congruent with your values, your whole life gets out of balance. You cause yourself emotional stress. You become angry and frustrated. You lash out at people around you. You become short-tempered and irritable. You will suffer from insomnia. Being out of balance too long will cause you to get colds, flu, and other ailments. Severe imbalance can lead to life-threatening illnesses, such as heart attacks, strokes, and even cancer. For these reason, it's vitally important that you clarify your values and then live by them.

Your Self-Image

The second part of your self-concept is your *self-image*. Your self-image is the way you see yourself in the present moment. Your self-image is made up of three parts: how you see yourself, how others see you, and how you *think* others see you.

These three may all be different. You may see yourself in a certain way and you may think others see you in a different way. And then, others may see you differently from your perceptions.

You always perform on the outside consistent with the mental picture that you have of yourself on the inside. If you see yourself as positive, happy, confident, competent, and capable in your life and your work, you'll behave like this on the outside in everything you do.

You can always tell what your self-image is, in any area of your life, by explaining how you feel when you're with people. A person with a positive self-image is relaxed and confident with others. A person with a negative self-image feels insecure and inferior with others, especially with people that he or she feels are ahead of him or her or better in some way.

Strive for Complete Alignment

Here's the interesting thing about your self-image. When the way you see yourself, the way others see you, and the way you think others see you are all the same, you feel great about yourself. Your self-image becomes completely integrated, like two sets of fingers coming together to form one set of folded hands.

The more you live your life consistent with your values and ideals, the more integrated your self-image will be and the better you will perform at everything you attempt.

Your Self-Esteem

The third part of your self-concept is your self-esteem. Your self esteem can be defined as how much you like yourself and respect yourself. It's your *reputation* with yourself. It's how you think about yourself relative to the rest of the world. It's the emotional component of your self-concept and is more important than any other factor.

Your level of self-esteem determines how enthusiastic and excited you feel, how happy you feel, how positive you feel, how well you get along with other people, and your overall level of satisfaction.

Psychologists have come to the virtually unanimous conclusion that your self-esteem is the real measure and monitor of your personality.

Psychologists have come to the virtually unanimous conclusion that your self-esteem is the real measure and monitor of your personality. How much you like yourself largely determines everything that happens to you in your interactions and relationships with others.

Be the Best You Can Be

And what is the key to high self-esteem? The key is simply this: when your behaviors and your values are consistent with each other, your self-esteem goes up. When your ideals and values are clear and when the qualities and behaviors that you most admire are the same qualities and behaviors that you practice with others, you like yourself better. You respect yourself more. You feel happier.

Whenever your inner world and your outer world are in alignment, whenever your activities and your values are congruent, and whenever your activities are in balance with the highest values that you hold, you feel terrific and perfectly centered in your life.

If you say and do one thing but you admire and respect another set of behaviors, you feel unhappy and dissatisfied. You feel out of balance. You feel a sense of incongruence.

To enjoy a sense of balance and equilibrium in your life, to feel happy and fulfilled and functioning at your very best is not easy. It requires effort. It requires that you think through who you really are and who you really want to be. Achieving balance requires that you do more of the things that are consistent with the actions of the very best person that you can imagine yourself becoming and that you stop doing and saying the things that are inconsistent with your highest ideals and aspirations.

Decide Your Values in Each Area

You achieve a better sense of balance by first of all determining your values in each area of your life. Define your values regarding your health, your relationships, your work, your interactions with other people, and money. Then examine your behaviors, the things you do, and honestly identify the things that you're doing and saying that are *not* consistent with these values. Then resolve to change them, one by one. In bringing your behaviors into alignment with your convictions, you start to feel wonderful about yourself. You start to feel more in balance. You start to feel happier and healthier and in alignment with the best elements of your character and personality.

Just as a car with perfectly aligned and balanced wheels runs smoothly down the highway, you will also run more smoothly down the highway of your life when you've taken the time and made the effort to bring everything that you do and say into balance and alignment with the very best person you can possibly be.

Summary

More people are going to make more money in business in the next few years than in all the years of human history. Your goal should be to be one of the big money earners. What you have learned in this book shows you how to do it.

No one is better than you and no one is smarter. Every master was once a beginner. Every successful businessperson started at the bottom and worked his way up. Everyone in the top 10 percent of people in your field today was at one time not in your field at all and didn't even know it existed. And whatever hundreds of thousands and even millions of other people have done, you can do as well.

All business skills are *learnable*. All money-making skills are learnable as well. You can learn any skill you need to learn to achieve any business or financial goals you can set for yourself.

You are now firmly launched on the road to wealth. There are no limits except the ones you place on yourself. Go for it!

Action Exercises

1. What are your three most important personal values? What do you stand for and believe in?

2. What are your three most important business values? What principles do you practice with your customers and in the operation of your business?

3. What are your three most important business goals, right now?

4. What are your three most important personal and family goals, right now?

5. What are your three most important health goals, right now?

6. What three virtues, values, or qualities do you want to be known for sometime in the future?

7. What three specific actions are you going to take immediately based on your answers to the above questions?

INDEX

Index

K
Key objections, 50
Kiosks, 115
Krispy Kreme Doughnuts, 118

L
Labor costs, 77–78, 151
Law of attraction, 102
Law of correspondence, 102, 220–221
Law of indirect effect, 69, 70
The Law of Success, 72
Law of the lid, 102
Law of three, 82–86
Leadership
  psychology of, 101–103
  relation to profits, 208
  of teams, 93
Lead generation and conversion,
  183–184
Learning organizations, 209–210
Levering, Robert, 215
Lexus, 141
Lid, law of, 102
Lifetime value of customers, 162–163
Locations (business)
  appearance of, 142–144
  new models for, 106–107
  questions for selecting, 112–122
  role of convenience in selecting,
    109–111
  in small versus large towns,
    111–112
Locations for job interviews, 83–84
Longevity, 222–225
Long-term view, 201
Loss leader pricing, 162–163
Low-profit items, 180–182
Luxury car sales, 141–142

M
Mailing sales information, 30
Malls, 116
Management by wandering around,
  205–206

Market-clearing price, 153–154
Market demand pricing, 163
Market pricing model, 158
Mastermind groups, 72–76
Maxwell, John, 102
McDonald's, 5, 11
Meeting and exceeding expectations,
  206–207
Meetings, 94–95, 206
Mercedes-Benz, 11
Mile of Cars, 116–117
Minor points, basing purchases on, 51
Misrepresentation, 8
Mission, 196–197
Mission statements, 227
Mistakes, 195
Money as motivator, 89–90
Monopoly prices, 158–159
Morale, 215–216
Motivating employees, 89–90
Motor home sales, 56–57
Motorola, 209
Mrs. Fields cookies, 108–109
Multiple of total costs model, 157

N
National City, 116–117
Navy blue, 137
Negative self-image, 229
Negativity, 221
Net margin, 167
Networking skills, 69–70
Newspaper advertising, 96–97
No-profit items, 180–182
Nordstrom, 11
Nutrition, 222–223

O
Objections, discovering, 50
Objectives, 91–92, 202–203
Offices, 142–144
Online commerce, 122
Order sheet close, 61
Outside service costs, 151

Index